Greg Giraldo

Greg Giraldo

A Comedian's Story

Matt Balaker

Wayne Jones

Starkbill Publishing

ISBN 978–1-7335924–0-6 (paperback)
ISBN 978–1-7335924–1-3 (ebook)
ISBN 978–1-7335924–2-0 (audiobook)

Library of Congress Control Number: 2019900084

General editing by Dorothea Halliday
Book design, production editing, and proofreading by Sheryl Holmberg

First published 2019

Cataloging Data
Balaker, Matt, 1978-
Greg Giraldo : a comedian's story / Matt Balaker, Wayne Jones
 p. cm.
Includes list of sources and index.
1. Giraldo, Greg, 1965–2010. 2. Comedians — United States — Biography.
3. Actors — United States — Biography. I. Jones, Wayne, 1959- . II. Title.
PN2287

Starkbill Publishing
Laguna Beach, California

starkbill.com

This book is dedicated to Greg's fans

Contents

Foreword

Reading this book has made me happy and sad for a man and a city that no longer exist, a time and place in New York where a guy like Greg Giraldo could grow into what he became. From Francis Lewis Boulevard in Queens to Regis High School to Columbia U to Harvard, he was a success story by anyone's standards, a working-class kid who tossed away a big law career to pursue what he was meant to do. Standup comedy. And he excelled in our thing, too. A funny brilliant mind that stood out in a field with a lot of funny brilliant minds.

And hearing everybody talking about how much they loved him and remembering the way I'd feel so glad when he showed up at the Comedy Cellar or on *Tough Crowd* — it all came flashing back to me. He was charming and friendly but also a fierce guy in many ways, but not in a stupid way. It was a ferocious thirst for knowledge and humor and meaning. And it ended pointlessly and needlessly.

It's a tragic story, I guess, but not really. It's a wonderful story with a tragic ending. And this book is great because it's a celebration of who and what Greg was.

Colin Quinn

Introduction

"Every day there's a story in the paper about how shitty our schools are," Greg Giraldo tells the crowd. Although he has performed this bit hundreds of times, his delivery comes off as instinctive and unrehearsed. With his right hand gripping the microphone, he pauses for a beat, and continues.

"I read a book—it was filled with letters that soldiers during the Civil War had written to their girlfriends back home. These guys were kids—they were 14-, 15-year-old kids. Most of these guys had never even been to school. But every single letter in the book was incredible."

The onlookers go quiet for a moment as Greg alters his voice to mimic an exaggerated 19th-century Southern accent.

"My dearest Hannah. This morn finds me wracked by the fiery pangs of your absence."

Laughter builds and quickly spreads throughout the Comedy Works audience. Before letting the chuckles subside, Greg continues: "I'll bear your cherished memory with me as I battle the forces of tyranny and oppression."

Speaking in his natural, slightly raspy New York tone, Greg says: "Now think about what the typical letter from your average modern-day soldier to his girlfriend back home in like New Jersey's gotta read like."

Adopting a New Jersey accent, Greg continues: "Dear Marie. It is hot as fuck out here."

Applause mixes with laughs, and he resumes: "It is hard to fight these sand monkeys wit' your balls stuck to your legs. It is very, very hot out here because I am in the *dessert*."

Acknowledging the intentional mispronunciation of *desert*, the fans reward Greg with an extended applause break. Back in character, Greg punctuates the joke: "What else did I want to *axe* you? Oh yeah, don't fuck nobody till I get back."

That evening in April 2006, Greg recorded the comedy special *Good Day to Cross a River*. As a nationally touring, headlining comedian, Greg had the admiration of other comics and a budding fan base. He no longer needed a day job. He was a professional comedian on the ascent with more than a decade of experience.

But it didn't start this way.

Chapter 1

The Smart Kid

Somebody as smart and bestowed with as many gifts as he, to still be that humble and unassuming is rare.
— Ted Alexandro

It took many years of practice, both in writing and performing, before the working-class kid made his way from Queens to several of the most prestigious stages in America. There were numerous highlights along the way. At times, he was able to suppress his own doubt long enough to convince himself that he had "made it." There were many low points too. He endured episodes of feeling depressed or frantic — even questioning whether he was in the right business. He benefited from a stellar education, but not in the way that he had anticipated, and certainly not in the manner that his parents had hoped for him. He matured into a warm-hearted adult and a much-appreciated friend. His fans regarded him as a masterful writer and a fearless performer.

All that and much more were decades in the distance when Gregory Carlos Giraldo was born on December 10, 1965, in the Queens borough of New York City. He grew up in a close-knit, Roman Catholic home with his two younger siblings — a brother, John, and a sister, Elizabeth — and their parents. Greg's mother, Dolores, lived in Spain before emigrating to the United States. Alfonso,

Greg's father, was born in Colombia and worked as a fuel-purchasing manager at Pan Am Airlines.

Greg's parents spoke only Spanish at home, and most of their family friends conversed in it as well. Greg heard English on television and on the play-grounds and streets of Jackson Heights, Queens, but nowhere else until he entered school. The dual lin-guistic heritage was a boon in practical terms, as Greg became totally at ease in both languages and gained knowledge of two foreign cultures — not to mention the American one that he was born into. Greg entered kindergarten in St. Kevin Catholic School in Flushing, Queens, at the age of four. He had no trouble assimilating into the English-speaking curriculum. He excelled, and his achieve-ments paid off.

Alfonso and Dolores had high aspirations for their precious son. When Greg became a teenager, they applied successfully for his acceptance into Regis High School, an elite, all-male, private Jesuit school in Manhattan, one of the most prestigious secondary schools in the nation. Tuition was free for all students thanks to the bequest from Regis's founder and to ongoing alumni donations. That was 1979 and Greg's parents were very proud. His straight A's from grade school, his entrance test, his interviews with the Regis faculty — all contributed to making Greg one of the 10 percent of applicants who got in.

Regis was located on 84th Street on the Upper East Side of Manhattan between Madison and Park Avenues—just blocks from the Metropolitan Museum of Art and Central Park. The building, an imposing structure built around a quad, extended an entire block. Regis's curriculum emphasized the classics. Greg studied literature, history, theology, philosophy, science, advanced math, art and music, and languages, including Latin. The same Greg with the scintillating language skills on the standup stage 20 years later was already burgeoning here. He not only read the epic poem the *Iliad* by the Greek author Homer, but he also translated a Latin version into English.

In the midst of all the seriousness, Greg and his classmates had ample opportunities to have fun. They enjoyed a fairly uncloistered social life. Greg and his friends hung out in the quad during lunchtime and after class. Seniors could leave the quad for lunch any day, the juniors only on Fridays, though many students broke that rule. If Greg got in trouble for returning late from lunch or breaking the dress code, he would receive detention, which involved sitting in a classroom after school, writing conciliatory phrases, and eagerly watching the clock. When he wasn't in class, Greg enjoyed going to concerts. He would see blues bands, rock groups, pretty much any ensemble with a guitar player. The genre didn't matter too much. He loved live music.

Jim Livio, a student at Regis at the time, remembered the music scene: "It was a cool time to be in New York City. Punk and New Wave were big. Bars and clubs were [plentiful], the drinking age was 18 — and nobody drove anywhere. You would take a cab or the subway, so there were no worries about drinking and driving."

Even with all this amusement, Greg did well at Regis. Journalist Robert Kurson wrote:

> *Once inside, Greg tore up the place. Shunning nerdiness, he pulled A's without losing his affection for the word* fuck *or his taste for the off-color joke. He read great literature, not because he was an egghead, but because Swift and Shakespeare were damn funny guys who knew how to construct a joke. His classmates dug his memory for* Saturday Night Live *dialogue, and they'll still tell you that his Eddie Murphy impressions were scary good. The Jesuits — great teachers, to Greg's mind — appreciated passion in a student, whatever the passion, so no one panicked about the joke-and-gag notebooks Greg continued to assemble.*

As a teenager, Greg was more innocent than he let on to his friends. He played soccer and refereed games on the weekends. Both of his parents instilled traditional values in their children. At home, Greg would not curse around his mother. He looked out for his younger sister.

Alfonso, a loving and strict influence, wanted his boys to be well-mannered gentlemen. Greg listened. "He was such a good boy," commented a girl who knew him in high school.

Greg had to leave Regis's campus to meet girls, including the ones who volunteered at the Lenox Hill Hospital, a half mile south of the school. He hit it off with Pauline Glaser, who set Greg's best friend up with her friend Jill. Greg connected with Glaser and her friends in a way he couldn't with his Regis classmates.

"We were religious Jewish and they were religious Catholic," Glaser said about her early interactions with Greg. "We always had discussions about what religions believe and what they don't . . . We'd discuss all the Jewish/Catholic stuff. It was interesting."

Glaser's mother had an inkling that her daughter was spending time with non-Jewish boys. "Don't go out with him," said Glaser's mother about Greg, who felt similar pressures at home about dating outside his religion. The teenagers did not heed their parents' advice. During their senior year, 1982, Greg and Glaser enjoyed a clandestine romance. Greg played an important role in helping Glaser cope with difficult adolescent struggles. "He was the nicest, sweetest guy, just a wonderful person," Glaser said about her time with Greg. "And he was funny."

Greg's friend proved to be a valuable wingman. Early one evening during their senior year of high school, the two of them hung out in a lively Queens neighborhood where several college students lived. They noticed two attractive women about to board a bus. After mustering up some courage, Greg blurted out to the girls: "If you get off the bus, we'll give you a ride wherever you want to go."

"Okay," they replied. Greg was surprised.

The four of them went out for drinks that night. Greg took an interest in Robin Lazarus, a vibrant New Yorker one year older than he was.

Soon thereafter, Greg and Robin started to date. Like many teenagers, Greg and Robin went to movies and dinners, but they also attended comedy shows on occasion. "We would argue about who was funnier," said Robin. While Robin lacked the desire to tell jokes in front of a room full of strangers, she noticed that Greg had a performer's mentality. "He always wanted to be out there," she said. "He always wanted to be something."

As they continued to date, Robin was amused by how Greg tried to hide his nerdy side. He wanted to be cool more than he wanted to be smart. Greg's charm worked, and the two enjoyed a fairly drama-free relationship. However, a snowstorm in mid-February created a tense moment for the young couple. On Valentine's Day in 1983, a massive snowfall hit New York City. Instead of taking Robin out to a romantic dinner, Greg decided to shovel snow off his neighbors' driveways to make some extra money.

Greg's opportunism didn't sit well with Robin. *What a dick,* she thought. Robin, upset with the circumstances, told Greg: "It's Valentine's Day, you're my boyfriend. What good is it having a boyfriend if I can't hang out with him on Valentine's Day?"

They made up and later that year Greg took Robin to his senior prom at the Waldorf Astoria, an iconic hotel in Manhattan. In 1983, Greg graduated from Regis and enrolled at Columbia University, about three miles away.

At Columbia, the students, most from affluent homes, came from a wide range of religions and cultures. Free thought was celebrated. Greg's best friend from Regis roomed with him in the Carman Hall dormitory, which helped ease Greg's transition to college life. Just down the hall from Greg lived Art Miller, a civil engineering student from Pennsylvania. Greg and Miller quickly became friends. Early in their freshman year, Greg, his roommate, and Miller befriended a group of fun-loving frat boys from the Psi Upsilon house. All three of them ultimately joined the Psi Upsilon fraternity. Perhaps it was the rituals, the songs, the traditions, but Greg developed a deep camaraderie with his frat brothers. Several of them studied engineering and science. These young men were some of the most academically advanced in the country. Yet they spent many afternoons hanging out at the Lambda house on 114th Street, pining about how to meet girls and discovering new ways to get drunk.

"We were big drinkers, smokers, whatever we could get our hands on, which was not much since we were broke college students," said Miller. "Mostly we drank beer, smoked pot, and played music." They also had an enterprising business sense. Greg and his Psi U brothers ran a campus beer distributorship out of the house.

For Greg, college life centered on Psi U. This house resonated with his outgoing sensibilities and provincial inclinations. Like Greg, the fraternity had a blue-collar, Queens-type vibe. Roughly half of its members had gone to Regis High School. They often saw themselves as outsiders from the wrong backgrounds at this uppity Ivy League institution. The fraternity gave them refuge. It was an authentically urban group—not like the kids from the suburbs who faked it: these guys had grown up in cities. They had street smarts and book smarts. Howard Stern played frequently on the house stereos. Copies of the *New York Post* piled high on unkempt coffee tables. Tap beer flowed freely. The house was a total shithole. And they loved it.

Like many college kids on the cusp of adulthood, they pranked each other, fought occasionally, and had a blast hanging out together. They were not above childish fun like shooting water balloons off the roof into the quad. The quad was a rich source of material for Greg. He liked to plug a microphone into his guitar amplifier and place it against an open bedroom window. Then he would scare unsuspecting students below, claiming to be the voice of God and offering silly messages of condemnation or playful ridicule. His friends found it hilarious.

Greg spent a great deal of his free time at the frat house. One evening after a long night of partying, Greg fell asleep on a bar-room chair while holding a drink in his hand. He stayed there till 4 a.m. when he was awoken by a large rat scampering on his lap. It tried to sip his beer. Greg pushed the rodent away. A few years later, the building was condemned and renovated.

Greg was their leader, first for the freshman class and then the whole fraternity — eventually serving as Psi Upsilon president. His peers called him "extraordinary," "brilliant," and appreciated his loyalty. Although popular, Greg wasn't afraid of an occasional tussle, and he knew how to throw a punch. In some instances, arguments would turn physical. Greg's tough-guy side earned him more respect among his friends, and he enjoyed bragging about it too. With his guitar skills and slightly rebellious attitude, Greg came off as more of a rock star than a comedian.

Some of the other musically inclined fraternity members teamed up with Greg to form a band. They lacked a name and a lengthy set list, but this makeshift rock band helped stoke Greg's love of performing. Greg played lead guitar. Most of their music was shared only with those that could hear them jam from the basement of the Psi U house. After their first gig, vandals stole their gear. But they regrouped for a second, and final, performance at the steps of the Low Memorial Library on campus.

The enclaves bordering the university were not always safe spaces, but the grittier aspects of city life didn't intimidate Greg. He visited his family on many weekends and often escaped to Francis Lewis Boulevard. "Franny Lew" was a roadway about nine miles east of Greg's hometown, and it was known for drag racing and nighttime cruising. To Greg, it provided a respite from school. He could relax there and enjoy himself with neighborhood friends.

Greg and Robin's relationship faded during his first year in college. The couple gradually drifted apart, eventually losing touch. But Greg didn't stay single for long. While helping some first-year Barnard students move into their dorm rooms, Greg caught the eye of an attractive young co-ed named Sue Gehm, who studied at Barnard before becoming a dental student at Columbia. She had also grown up in Queens. The two began a relationship that would become more serious in their years after college.

Greg's extracurricular activities extended beyond the frat house. He played club soccer for a year and mentored neighborhood children. He volunteered several hours each week as part of Big Brothers and Sisters NYC, a charitable organization that fostered one-on-one relationships with mentors and adolescents in underserved communities. Greg approached his volunteerism with a sense of humor. Concerned with the language shortcomings of one of the boys—Greg said the kid spoke "fucked-up English and fucked-up Spanish"—Greg helped the boy improve. Although Greg understood what the boy meant in either language, he had great sympathy for him and his poorly developed communication skills. Greg's bilingualism helped the boy enhance his verbal capabilities.

Columbia's Ivy League rigor was no major obstacle for Greg. A love of reading made majoring in English a natural choice. Regis had prepared him well. Greg studied and attended class. But he was not always a model student. He lapsed occasionally. After sleeping too late, Greg said: "I probably should have taken my history exam this morning." Missing the test bothered Greg; however, he masked his disappointment with nonchalance. At times cavalier about schoolwork, Greg aced most of his classes. He didn't need to study for hours or cram for each midterm to get a high grade point average. He could do well without taking academics too seriously.

Around junior year, Greg's mentors suggested he apply to law school as they did to most students who were gifted in language and the humanities. He didn't have a clear idea of what he wanted to do after college. So he signed up to take the Law School Admission Test (LSAT). With little preparation, Greg earned a near-perfect score, putting him in the top one percent of test takers.

Greg graduated from Columbia in 1987, and as he put it, felt "dragged along by fate" to enter Harvard Law School. Law school was a default choice rather than a lifelong passion for Greg. Some of his Columbia friends teased him about his academic choice. "How come everyone's acting like I sold out?" he asked. Downplaying his acceptance, Greg told his friends that Harvard needed another Hispanic. Greg entered Harvard a year before another famous alumnus, Barack Obama, who had allegedly scored five to 10 percentage points lower on the LSAT than Greg had.

In the summer of 1987, Greg hopped in the car with his parents for the 200-mile drive from Queens, New York, to Cambridge, Massachusetts. Alfonso and Dolores beamed with pride and eagerly anticipated seeing the Harvard campus. They arrived at Harvard Law School and helped Greg move into his new living quarters—a humble suite with three bedrooms and one bathroom in each unit. Greg's parents seemed a bit surprised at the living conditions for some of the smartest students in the world. They may have expected Harvard Law School to have newer and better-quality dorms. Nonetheless, they were incredibly happy for Greg and excited about the beginning of his law school education.

Dave Diamond, a friendly and witty first-year student from San Diego County who had recently graduated from UC Berkeley, was in one of the bedrooms alphabetizing cassette tapes. Greg had fun with their first interaction. After he introduced himself and his parents to Diamond, he said, "They don't speak English."

Greg was messing with his new roommate — both his parents knew English. With the help of his mother and father, Greg unpacked his belongings. He hugged Dolores and Alfonso, who said goodbye to "Guapo," a loving nickname meaning *handsome* in Spanish. The couple then drove back to New York.

Later that week, Greg had to find an outfit for an evening event. Harvard Law School was throwing a get-acquainted cocktail party. Greg rarely had occasion to dress in formal wear. He scoured the town for what he assumed to be the staple of high-fashion evening wear — the blue blazer. He apparently found one with zippers to wear to the gathering.

When Greg first arrived at Harvard, he made an effort to fit in. He attended class regularly and studied diligently. Even though he was highly educated, he felt somewhat insecure among the accomplished and capable students that surrounded him. At times, Greg lamented that he wasn't good enough or smart enough or even that he was an imposter and no match for the astronauts, politicians, and many

Rhodes Scholars in his class. He confided to a friend that he felt that his Harvard classmates thought he had gotten in based on affirmative action and not on his own merits. Greg's buddy shot this down immediately and said that once people talked with him for five minutes, they knew that he was one of the most intelligent people they had ever met. Nonetheless, Greg felt like an outsider at Harvard.

Greg loved music. Throughout his life, he enjoyed a wide variety, from acts like the Black Crowes, Guns N' Roses, and Lucinda Williams — to, later in life, acts like the Raconteurs, Ike Reilly, and the Nocturnals. At Harvard, Greg's listening tastes were still somewhat limited, but Diamond helped expand Greg's musical palate when he popped in one of his many cassette tapes.

"What's that?" Greg asked.

"It's the Smiths," Diamond said.

Greg replied, "Oh, you know, I don't think I've ever actually listened to them." This surprised Diamond since the Smiths were one of the most popular bands of the '80s. Apparently, some of Greg's friends in Queens had joked that listening to the Smiths called one's heterosexuality into question.

Greg asked to borrow the tape, and a few days later he broke out his guitar and started to play "This Charming Man" in his room. Diamond, who happened to be walking by, noticed Greg strumming the Smiths' hit.

14

Greg, surprised to see his roommate, joked, "You know what? They really don't seem that gay."

Diamond responded, "Well, they do when *you* play them."

Greg and Diamond were friends from that day on.

Life as a Harvard Law student was intense. Kurson, who also attended Harvard Law, remembered that the students were smart and highly competitive: "The intellect there was staggering, but even worse than that was the ambition. You were in this pool of ravenous sharks, all of whom were looking to destroy you."

The upside, though, was that it wasn't in the interest of the university for any student to fail. Kurson said that if you managed to get into Harvard Law in the first place, you were going to graduate: "It was going to take almost an act of God to flunk out because Harvard did not like to do that. It did not like to have on its record that it had failed in selecting."

Harvard Law School put on several social events to welcome students and help remind them that they were surrounded by scholastic high-fliers. One such affair occurred during Greg's first year and featured performances by comedians who worked in Boston clubs. Greg was already known among some of the students, even early on, for being "particularly sharp and funny." Greg sized up the professional comedians.

One of the comics imitated Johnny Most, the radio voice for the Boston Celtics: "The comedian was doing a really interesting impression of Johnny Most . . . a re-creation of a play-by-play of a Celtics-Lakers game," said Kurson. "He was saying that Kurt Rambis just stabbed Larry Bird because Johnny Most would always go over the top in his homerism." That comedian was Mike Donovan, who remembered the format of the show:

> *It was a mock courtroom where the students learned the law in a physical replica of a real courtroom . . . It was a two-man 30–30 show [30 minutes each] and the opener was Mike Moto . . . There were about 400 students, but the sprinkling of the professors here and there with their bowties and tweed jackets was what made it as unique as the fact of the physical room itself . . . The professors were cool but the students did the laughing . . . Moto did a strong opening set. I did better, but I do remember now that the Johnny Most kicked the whole thing into high gear. It's a 5-minute closing bit where the Celtics' biased announcer is red-in-the-face mad at the refs in 40 ways.*

There were other events with other celebrities, including Whoopi Goldberg, Ed Asner, and Rae Dawn Chong, and these were likely attended by Greg as well, said Kurson.

When Greg first started law school, he made a concerted effort to attend Harvard-led social events. But this changed quickly, and he went to fewer law school mixers. He found it more enjoyable to venture into Boston and hang out with "real people."

He made it through his first year and managed to land a summer job at a small law firm. It was common for most of his classmates to work for law firms during their summer breaks, even if they weren't interested in becoming lawyers, because the pay was good and the duties were light. These summer internships required little actual office work from Greg. They were easy assignments and helped law firms recruit new candidates. His duties included going to baseball games, concerts, and parties.

The summer program Greg entered was more of a social mixer than real preparation for law firm life: the main idea was to see if people liked you, "and [likeability] was Greg's biggest, strongest quality. You knew it the second you met him." The law firms wanted the Harvard students to like the place as well, and the way they achieved that was not by working the students hard but by showing them a good time so that in the end they felt they belonged there.

In the summer of 1988, Greg and Diamond moved with their friend Matt Paroly, a former English major at the University of Michigan, and one other roommate, Gary Sheff, into a four-bedroom apartment in Somerville, about a mile and a half north of campus, near Porter Square. The dwelling lacked decorative touches or luxurious amenities. Saran Wrap on the windows helped insulate the place from the cold Somerville winters. There were two large rooms. The living room housed the television, couch, and two chairs. The dining room was unique. Greg and his friends didn't expect to use a dining table, so they opted for a ping-pong table instead. The tight space made maneuvering around the table difficult. The small room allowed for only about three or four feet of space around the table. They remarked that it was like arena ping-pong.

The roommates engaged in frequent ping-pong battles. Greg's long, gangly arms gave him a competitive advantage. During one of their more intense marathons, Greg lost a point to Diamond. Upset, Greg threw his paddle at the wall. It cut through the cheap drywall and landed in Diamond's bedroom. They used this event to develop a running joke that became more elaborate over time. They made up a story that Barack Obama was playing ping-pong with them and got so pissed off when Diamond beat him that Obama threw the paddle through the wall and shouted, "This is the last time I'll ever lose to a Jew in my life!" The future U.S. president never did play ping-pong at their place. This fabricated story became an ongoing joke between Greg and Diamond, who found it especially hilarious when others repeated it back to them years later thinking it was true.

Greg got along well with his roommates. They joked with one another, but Greg never sought the spotlight. He didn't try to stick out with his humor. All four of them were funny. Paroly said: "We all would sit around and have a conversation where we'd ad lib and be funny and laugh . . . But he was not a performer; he was not a comedian at that point." Greg kept an unassuming attitude towards others. During law school, he rarely came off as pushy or overconfident. However, he could drop his soft-spoken demeanor under certain circumstances.

One night Greg went out with his roommates to a popular Harvard Square bar and Chinese restaurant called the Hong Kong. The venue was popular for its Scorpion Bowls—oversized drinks served in large noodle bowls with giant straws. There was enough in one bowl for two people. These colorful libations were ideal for getting drunk quickly. After downing some Scorpion Bowls upstairs, Greg and his pals encountered four loud-mouthed partiers— not from Harvard. They created an obnoxious scene. One guy bumped Greg, and said, "Hey, what's your fucking problem, buddy?"

Greg's Queens-tough-guy persona came out. "I don't have a problem," Greg shouted back. "You got a problem?" Now closer to the instigator, Greg said, "You want to fuck with me? I'll fuck with you."

Paroly and Diamond, trying to diffuse the tension, said to Greg: "Whoa, whoa, whoa! Chill out!"

The conflict de-escalated. After some posturing, the group of townies went downstairs. Greg, still fuming from the altercation, cooled off with his friends at the bar. It appeared the skirmish had ended. Greg and his buddies decided to leave. However, once outside, Greg confronted the same group of tough guys.

The argument reignited. Greg and the group leader went at it. Their tempers flared. "I'm going to fuck you over, you fucking idiot!" Greg yelled. "You get the fuck out of here!"

The scuffle didn't last long. One of the men grew tired of the trash talk and sucker-punched Greg without warning. He went down immediately. Greg knocked his head against a parked car before passing out on the icy sidewalk.

An ambulance arrived quickly, and paramedics tended to Greg, who appeared to suffer from a concussion.

"What year is it?" asked an emergency medical technician. "1984," Greg said, off by four years.

"Who's the president?" inquired the paramedic. "Some asshole," Greg responded.

The emergency crew placed Greg on a gurney and rushed him to the hospital, where he received stitches. Several hours later, Greg returned home. "I can't believe that guy beat me up," Greg said.

Paroly replied, "Greg, nobody beat you up. His friend coldcocked you out of nowhere and then you hit your head on the side of a car, cut your temple open, and went down like a sack of potatoes."

Greg kept his sense of humor about the incident. He joked that the fight would be called the Sweet and Sour Chicken Ass Kickin' — a play on Rumble in the Jungle, the famous heavyweight title match between Muhammad Ali and George Foreman.

Greg's friendship with his Somerville roommates involved more than ping-pong and bar fights. The four shared similar outlooks on education and career planning. They never longed to join the *Harvard Law Review* or sit in the front of the class. They drank, overslept, and missed almost as many classes as they attended. However, they applied themselves and performed well when it mattered. "All of us were slackers but not to the point where we got bad grades," said Paroly. This included Greg, who did his work and passed his courses. He had his own way of studying. Greg littered his room with notebooks, index cards, and mountains of paper. It looked like a disorganized mess. Nevertheless, it worked for Greg. He could access what he needed. All the material was within his reach. The four apartment-mates didn't have clearly defined ideas of what they wanted to do after law school. Greg embraced the uncertainty. Law school served as a three-year exploratory period.

Throughout his time at Harvard, Greg thought much about the sacrifices his parents had made to help him get there. They weighed on him. Greg knew that his law school experience wasn't living up to what he thought his mother and father imagined. During one of his all-nighters, Greg shared with his roommates that he felt guilty for putting off the assignment until the night before it was due. Greg said, "My dad would be so mortified if he knew."

In the summer of 1989, Greg took another summer internship in New York City. During this time, he befriended Leslie Adler, a student at Brooklyn Law School. Adler was fascinated to meet Greg and so many Ivy Leaguers. Greg's fun-loving attitude made him of one the most popular in the group of summer associates.

"We had a wild summer," Adler said. "This was before the markets crashed."

Greg brought his girlfriend, Sue Gehm, to many of the social events. And they had a wonderful time enjoying the city with other students and lawyers.

Not only was Greg well liked by the summer interns, but he also impressed several of the firm's full-time lawyers with his charisma and charm. His knack for building one-on-one connections resulted in less desk work and more outside excursions. "If you had a decent personality and were fun, you could be wined and dined," Adler said. "As long as full-time associates took you out, they could expense anything. I think that summer we saw every play and every concert that was playing in New York. We really had a ball."

The summer excitement ended, and Greg went back to Harvard for one more year. The notion of working full time at a stuffy mega-firm worried Greg. Still, he benefited from the broad curriculum and mental discipline that Harvard provided. His Ivy League education didn't focus on vocational preparation. Instead, it emphasized philosophy, rhetoric, and debate — subjects Greg would later put to good use.

Greg got through law school. While happy he had finished, he never viewed completing law school as his crowning achievement. Greg's time at Harvard was no magical experience. He didn't feel like part of the mainstream. He did graduate, though, in the late spring of 1990, and he would soon learn what life was like for a young attorney at one of New York City's top law firms.

Chapter 2
Lawyer and Comedian

Being a comic is a lot more fun than being a lawyer.
                                                    – Jim Norton

After graduating from Harvard, Greg started working in September 1990 at the same international law firm where he had worked during the previous summer—Skadden, Arps, Slate, Meagher & Flom, one of the most prestigious firms in New York. To many in the legal field, a Skadden pedigree carried more cachet than even a Harvard law degree.

Skadden gained prominence in the 1980s when the firm was at the epicenter of a fervent mergers and acquisitions market. The real estate and Wall Street booms helped Skadden generate record revenues. In 1985, it ranked as one of the country's top three largest law firms. Skadden lured young attorneys with its prestige and pay. Skadden practically built a pipeline from Harvard Law School. By the time Greg joined the firm, it had a sterling reputation, but money didn't roll in as fast as it had in the '80s heyday.

Greg's summer internships were an unrealistic prelude to the treacherous and cloistered career he had now embarked on. Life at big law firms in the '90s was a grind, not a job where Greg could phone it in. All-nighters were common. Those who worked more than 100 hours a week were praised by other lawyers in the hallways. Brainpower pervaded. Greg could use his entire vocabulary without appearing pompous.

Power partners, mostly overweight men, catered to executive clients of a similar ilk. Large bottles of Tylenol were displayed on mahogany desks like status symbols of the migraines the work caused. Other stronger and more addictive vices were hidden from sight. The chain of command was almost militaristic.

"This place looks like the *Star Wars* Death Star," Greg remarked as he looked up at the black windows of the 47-floor high-rise office building at 919 Third Avenue in Midtown Manhattan that housed Skadden.

Junior associates ate dinner at their desks and at times enjoyed drinks at P. J. Clarke's, one of New York City's oldest bars. New attorneys had the camaraderie of other young associates—a white-collar army of privates in a corporate foxhole of sorts. Greg disdained the power hierarchy but managed to have fun at Skadden.

Greg noticed a familiar face amid the sea of dress suits and file cabinets. Leslie Adler, his friend from the prior summer's internship, shared an office wall with him. The two reconnected, and Adler witnessed many of Greg's more infamous hijinks. Greg loved to make prank phone calls during work— including Coca-Cola's corporate offices.

"I soaked my toe in your soda for two days, and now it fell off," Greg lamented one afternoon to an unsuspecting Coke employee. "I want money or I'll sue."

Adler tried to hide her laughter from the Skadden partners. Greg didn't let an $85,000 annual salary crush his sense of humor.

Although Greg showed no signs of an accent when he spoke English, he spoke Spanish fluently. Adler knew this, so she asked Greg to help decipher a letter she had received from a cleaning lady in her building.

"We had no idea what the hell it meant," Adler said. "So I brought it to work, and he sat with it all day."

The note included a line that read, "E-E-S-A-B-R-O-Q-U-I-N."

Hours later, Greg walked into Adler's office and said, with a heavy Spanish accent, "Theesa masheena no working. It's a broken."

Greg said that he had figured it out when he decided to think like his parents and understand how somebody would write a letter in broken English. Greg and Adler cracked up.

Greg cultivated other important friendships at Skadden, including the one he had with Steve Klein, a tax attorney, who started in January 1991.

During Klein's first day at Skadden, Greg, who had never met him before, walked into Klein's office unannounced to offer an impromptu and faux-serious "welcome to the firm" speech. Greg expounded on his exaggerated affinity for the profession and phony admiration for Skadden. Klein laughed. The two 20-something lawyers quickly bonded.

Greg and Klein occasionally worked together on assignments. These included mortgage-backed transactions, leveraged buyouts, and other time-intensive, high-stakes matters. However, pro bono projects were included too. Greg teamed up with Klein on one such task. It had nothing to do with defending the disenfranchised or fighting injustice. A privileged woman, who was friendly with a Skadden partner, wanted help setting up a nonprofit related to her dance studio.

How the hell did we get this? Greg thought.

The two office neighbors gave minimal attention to what they considered a waste-of-time undertaking. The high-society lady was so unimpressed with their work that she fired them. Greg was let go by a client who paid nothing. Experiences like these helped sharpen Greg's ability to see multiple sides of an issue. *We're helping one bullshit corporation get the best of another bullshit corporation,* he thought. He understood the good and bad in most sides.

Greg's friendly demeanor and quick wit made him popular with other attorneys. He amused his colleagues with hilarious impressions of Skadden personnel, mostly partners. Steven Siegel, an attorney who had already worked at Skadden for a few years, appreciated Greg's creative side and love of music. Siegel stuck out to Greg because he had a guitar in his office, which he knew how to play. The two shared more than a passion for guitar: both disliked the notion that lawyers were easily substituted for one another, viewed as fungible assets. Each took a holistic view of law and disliked strict hierarchy.

Greg valued Siegel's friendship so much that he developed a spot-on impression of him. Siegel caught word of this from one of Greg's first-year colleagues and wanted to witness his mimicry in action. So Siegel cornered Greg one afternoon in the hall and said, "Greg, I hear you do a really funny impersonation of me."

Befuddled, Greg tried to avoid Siegel's request. But Siegel wouldn't give up. Soon a small crowd gathered. Greg looked at Siegel and said, "No, I'm not going to."

Siegel replied, "Come on, Greg. Come on. You know I got a sense of humor. Everybody here says you do a good impression of me."

"No."

"Come on, Greg. Do me!"

"No, Steve, I am not going to *do you*," Greg said.

The group of onlookers laughed, but Siegel never saw Greg's impression of him.

Brilliant in many ways, Greg was ill-suited for a career as a lawyer. In law school, he got by on his book smarts, but practicing law required keen attention to detail and relentless focus on organization—skills Greg lacked. And he knew it. Greg explained, "If you spend five minutes with me or watch me try to balance my checkbook, you can only imagine the disaster I would make of anyone's legal issues." Greg would occasionally show up for assignments with the wrong client's files. One of his closest friends called Greg the most disorganized person he had ever met.

Real estate law was particularly inappropriate for him. Greg loathed poring through mountains of documents to analyze financial statements, lease agreements, title rights, and other deal minutiae. At Skadden, he would have to take orders from real estate partners before he could do any substantive legal work.

The desk work and the sterile office environment took a toll on Greg's psyche. Law firm drudgery ate at him. Reviewing documents and dealing with law firm politics nearly broke him. He needed an escape. On occasion, he would get a friend to keep the light on at his office to make the partners think he was working and leave the office in the late evenings to play guitar at bars and coffee houses in Queens.

Soon Greg's creative endeavors expanded beyond music, and he began flirting with standup comedy and acting. Greg was alerted to an acting opportunity for a part in a largely improvised play called Tony n' Tina's Wedding. He went for it.

Greg entered the theater holding a phony résumé he had written only one hour prior. Stapled to it was a poorly lit Polaroid picture of himself wearing a lawyer's suit. As he walked onto the chilly stage, a voice from the darkness blandly asked, "Can you tell us your name and which role you're auditioning for?"

"Uh, Greg Giraldo. Banquet manager." He was surprised by how nervous he felt.

Then another voice, a man's, shouted, "Whenever you're ready."

Greg placed his fake résumé on a stool next to him and improvised, making no reference to the fact that he was about 30 years younger than the character he was auditioning for. Greg's likeability carried him. Everyone in the room went crazy. He kept going with his unplanned material for several minutes, and at one point, he noticed one of the older men get up from his seat and whisper to another: "This guy's pretty funny." By the end of the audition, the producer and director were shaking his hand. An assistant took the résumé from the stool. As Greg left the theater, he decided to try that open mic night he had read about in the *Village Voice*.

Greg loved the comedy of Lenny Bruce and Richard Pryor as well as other icons. However, his urge to hit the stage had little to do with the greats. Rather, he felt motivated by watching some of the less-polished, more struggling comics on *Evening at the*

Improv. Greg thought, *I can do better than these guys.* And he scribbled more joke ideas in his notebook.

He started performing as an amateur at open mics and bringer shows. The audience at these shows consisted of typically polite and supportive friends of the comedians. Greg stood out from the other performers. "It was very clear he could do this from that moment," said Steve Klein. "I mean, he absolutely killed and, like, everybody's people were coming up to him after the show going, 'You can do this!'"

Open mics were hosted typically by an experienced comedian, but the other comedians were generally beginners and often first-time performers.

In bringer shows, amateur comedians bring their own audiences—literally. Each performer is required to bring a certain number of guests. It serves the dual purpose of giving comedians a chance to perform while ensuring the venue makes some money in the process.

Greg's first open-mic performance was likely at the New York Comedy Club, then located on the East Side, just over a mile south of Skadden's building at the time. He could easily get to the club from work.

Leslie Adler attended some of Greg's first standup shows, and she was blown away by Greg's intellect and precision on stage.

"He was good right away," Adler said.

Even at this early stage, Greg focused on preparation. He would read newspapers and come up with his own angles on current events.

The booming economy fizzled somewhat, and Skadden felt the pain. Several young lawyers were asked to leave. Skadden brought in career counselors to help the new attorneys identify their strengths and weaknesses, and based on his answers to the questions Greg realized that working at a large law firm was not for him. He hated it. Greg thought about Steve Klein's suggestion about pursuing comedy seriously.

Eventually, he reached his breaking point. One afternoon Greg broke the news to Adler. "I'm leaving," he said. "I don't want to do this anymore."

This confused Adler, who thought about all the student loans Greg owed. "I don't understand," she said to Greg. "I have a notebook," Greg said. "I write comedy."

Adler pleaded with Greg, "Why do you have to leave? Just go at night. You're so bored here anyway, and you don't really care to impress anyone with your work ethic, so just leave when you have to leave."

Adler's lobbying didn't change his mind. Greg's time at Skadden didn't last long. By 1991, about 10 months after his start date, Greg exited Skadden's offices for the last time. He grabbed his notebook and walked out the door.

Although Greg knew the law wasn't the right profession for him, he still had to figure out a way to pay his bills. Sue stayed on track with her dental career. Greg pondered what to do next. He continued to practice law in different roles. There were other jobs too, and most of them were forgettable. He worked in a haze, unsure of what to do next.

During this time of career turmoil, he took an important step forward in his personal life. On July 6, 1991, Greg and Sue got married at a small church in Queens. Both families celebrated the union. Neighborhood friends gathered to enjoy the lovely, understated festivities. Greg's wedding party included friends from high school, college, and law school. His younger brother, John, was the best man. Greg played guitar. He and Sue swayed to Eric Clapton's "Wonderful Tonight." Attendees danced, drank, and had a great time.

Greg supported Sue's dental aspirations. She graduated with a Doctor of Dental Surgery (DDS) degree in 1992, and he supplied a joking note of congratulations that was published in the yearbook of Columbia's School of Dental and Oral Surgery that year:

> *Congratulations!*
> *Dr. Susie the-tooth-driller Gehm*
>
> *I couldn't be prouder of you – not even if you had won the Nobel Peace Prize or captured the heavyweight boxing title. Well, maybe then. I mean,*

that would entail gaining a solid hundred twenty pounds of muscle mass and thousands of rounds of intense sparring.

You're the greatest.

Love,
Greg

However, the marriage didn't last long — only about a year. One of Greg's colleagues at Skadden recalled that Sue, while generally quite supportive of Greg's comedy overall, was less than enthusiastic about his lifestyle change. Greg was a different man in many ways than the teenager she had met years ago in college. He wanted to pursue standup, and she was a hard-working dentist.

During his initial foray into comedy, Greg befriended another aspiring comic. He and Greg were often the only two performers dressed in business attire. The comic was Jim Gaffigan, who had grown up in a large Irish Catholic family in Indiana before graduating from Georgetown University and taking an advertising job in New York City. Gaffigan would go on to become one of the most successful comedians of his era. Greg broke the news of his divorce to Gaffigan, who asked: "What are you doing?" Greg replied, "There are things I want to do."

Greg needed a day job to cover the high cost of living in New York City. Shortly after splitting up with Sue, he reached out to his close friend from

Columbia, Art Miller. Greg's fraternity brother ran a manufacturing business in Tribeca that served the construction industry. Miller gave Greg a job. Officially, Greg worked in the sales and administration department. However, his actual work consisted mostly of writing jokes and inviting Miller to his comedy shows. Greg did roll up his sleeves on one important undertaking. He spackled, sanded, and helped construct the Access Theater, an Off-Broadway venue devoted to assisting new artists. Greg's stint with Miller's firm soon ended.

In 1992 Greg reconnected with Steven Siegel. Greg began to work for him, first at his small law firm, Siegel and Levitt. Around June of that year, Greg jumped to a new opportunity with Siegel, a start-up tourist information company called RestQuest. Siegel, who had left Skadden in September 1991, genuinely liked Greg and respected his professional skills. "I obviously thought that he was a talented guy as it pertained to the law, as well as many other things," said Siegel, who had much in common with Greg.

They were both analytical and logical but also creative thinkers. "We never let the left side [of the brain] dominate," Siegel said.

RestQuest was located in a beautiful loft in New York's SoHo neighborhood. Glass partitions separated the elegant workspaces. Greg could come and go as he pleased. As long as the work was done, no one bothered him. These were the early days of the internet. The business was to compile and map vacation options.

A website described RestQuest as "an Internet company that harnessed new database search technologies." Greg remembered it differently: "I had this job at this weird travel company that my friend was starting, and there were just tons of hot girls that worked there. It was this bizarre company that he spent his life savings starting up, a company which was building a database of places you can go on vacation. It was supposed to be this great travel database, and literally the internet was just coming together. We got paid all this money to type vacation brochures into his database, and he thought he was going to have this unique searchable database. I said, 'I see some stiff competition right around the corner.'"

Greg's duties at RestQuest were broader than that, though. He served as an advisor as well, attending meetings and providing input to Siegel on a wide range of matters. RestQuest gained traction. The company partnered with Metro-North Railroad and Avis Rent A Car. *The Today Show* interviewed its management. Several publications wrote about it. The company had all the makings of a billion-dollar success story. However, the venture didn't last.

There were no seven-figure payouts for Greg and Siegel. In 1995, RestQuest shut its doors permanently.

Around this time, Greg first met comedian Nick Di Paolo, who allowed Greg to open for him at Catch a Rising Star in Princeton, New Jersey. "For a guy that had only been doing it a little while at that point, he seemed in command up there," said Di Paolo. "He had a presence about him and he was hip looking. His stuff was really funny. He seemed a little advanced. I could just see the potential. I could tell he was smart and had a lot of charisma. It was just obvious that he was going to go somewhere."

In the mid-1990s, Greg became friendly with Jessie Baade, another budding comedian in the local standup circuit. In 1994, she interviewed him at Chuckles in Mineola on Long Island for her self-produced comedy documentary. "The tape started because I wanted to do a documentary on the comedy scene in New York," Baade said. "I was well liked enough to get people to interview. I had good questions because I knew my subject. And I had a really shitty camera with no experience shooting it." Greg was respectful to Baade and other comedians in general.

"He was a gentleman," Baade said. "He was very aware that we were girls having to travel in, so he would give us a ride back. We would always have a really good time in the car because we were in a group with really funny people, so driving around was a novelty. It was also really fun."

Although early in his career, Greg had a veteran's stage presence—his poise and confidence seemed effortless. He smoothly weaved between written material and crowd work—the latter an especially uncommon skill for beginners.

Greg stood out from other novices. He tackled current events and personalized his material. Greg's delivery was fast and concise. His comedic instincts stood out to his peers, including Jon Stewart and Mike Sweeney, who became a longtime writer for Conan O'Brien. Greg didn't have a problem figuring out why something was funny—he knew it quickly. His smarts allowed him to develop bits on a wide range of topics. He had jokes about the turmoil in Ireland involving the Irish Republican Army, Protestants, and Catholics: "As far as I can tell, the only difference between Catholics and Protestants is that Catholics kneel during mass," Greg quipped. "That's where all this fighting in Ireland is from." In a thick Irish accent, Greg delivered the punch line, "Ya bloody kneel-lah, you!"

Greg also touched on First World problems. The Epstein-Barr virus—known to some as the yuppie flu—was a popular news story at the time. Greg said about the ailment, "You're very tired all the time and you can't get out of bed in the morning. Well, call me an ambulance. I'm in the late stages of that one."

In another bit, Greg mentioned that Roseanne Barr and Tom Arnold had announced that they would be moving to a farm. In response, Greg said that the only thing he could imagine them plowing through was pints of Häagen-Dazs ice cream. His skills at roasting, which he would go on to be famous for, showed even at this early stage.

Greg left law as a profession and took up comedy as a passion. He had hated working as a lawyer, but he didn't think standup would be his livelihood. Friends suggested that he marry his book smarts with his stage skills and become an entertainment executive.

Greg wanted no part of that. His legal training helped prepare him for the next phase of his professional life. Creating jokes was not entirely different from making legal decisions. He could present a point of view—justify it and defend it. He could recognize ambiguity and nuance. While Greg didn't want to publicize his legal background, its influence remained with him throughout his comedy career.

Chapter 3
Common Law: The Sitcom

*Most people who find out I'm Hispanic, they react the
same way: "Like, wow, man, you don't seem Hispanic."
They say it like it's an enormous compliment.*

— Greg Giraldo

Within five years of giving up a lucrative law career, Greg had established himself as a mainstay on
the standup comedy circuit. He toured throughout
the country, but New York City was his home base.
Greg caught the eye of a powerful entertainment
agent at a club in the city. This performance started
a sequence of events that changed his life forever.

In 1995 Carolines Comedy Club hosted a special
event for entertainment executives. It was an industry showcase. Comics would do short sets in hopes
of impressing the right people. Greg hated these
shows. He considered them a sham to get comics to
perform for free. He nonetheless agreed to do this
one. Cheryl Bayer from Creative Artists Agency
(CAA) was in the audience. CAA was a hugely influential agency. Its clients included David Letterman, Meryl Streep, Brad Pitt, and other A-listers.
Bayer watched Greg's set. She didn't speak to him
afterward, but it wasn't for lack of interest. She had
far greater plans for him.

Bayer walked straight to a Carolines manager
and asked, "Is Greg in the Montreal Festival?"

"No," said the manager.

"Well, he's in now," said Bayer. CAA had an open spot at the festival, and Greg filled it.

Greg signed with CAA and flew north to Canada. He took advantage of this opportunity. This was the place where a standout performance could dramatically affect a comedian's career. Nick Di Paolo said: "In the '90s at the Montreal Comedy Festival, everybody came home with a deal."

Rick Dorfman, Greg's close friend who worked with other Carolines comedians, became Greg's manager and accompanied him to Montreal.

Greg's performance at the New Faces show at the Montreal Comedy Festival killed. The postshow dealmaking began immediately at the bar of the Delta Hotel in downtown Montreal. It was a giant game of cat-and-mouse. Greg's team strategized to land the best deal possible. Bayer told Dorfman: "When I'm with Greg, come over and I'll introduce you to whoever I'm talking to. Then leave and come back with some made-up news. If it's a CBS exec, tell him that some guy from ABC wants to see Greg immediately."

Two weeks after Montreal, Greg and Dorfman flew to Los Angeles and stayed at the Wyndham Belage Hotel in West Hollywood. There, a mass of Hollywood executives tried to land a deal with Greg. Dorfman met with every network and production company rep he could. Network presidents called, begging for the chance to work with Greg.

NBC, ABC, and CBS all made offers. "It was wild. They were wining and dining us," said Dorfman.

Ultimately they went with Witt/Thomas and ABC. Witt/Thomas was a legendary production company that created several hit TV shows, including *Soap*, *The Golden Girls*, and *Nurses*. Dorfman received several scripts that he reviewed with Greg. They picked one for a show in which Greg played a lawyer.

The show's title was *Common Law* and it was produced by Warner Bros. in conjunction with Witt/Thomas. Producers cast the series around Greg, who played John Alvarez, the only Hispanic lawyer at a primarily white law firm in New York. Many of the details about Alvarez were derived from Greg's life: a guy from Queens who played the guitar and graduated from Harvard Law School. Even Alvarez's father, played by Gregory Sierra, was based on Greg's dad Alfonso.

The sitcom called for a strong female lead. Megyn Price, an appealing young actor, possessed the requisite brains and talent to match Greg's charm and intellect. Price met Greg during her final audition for the role of his girlfriend. The two hit it off immediately. During the audition, they improvised lines and amused each other with sarcastic ad libs. "He just had the best laugh of all time," said Price. Greg was comfortable around her. The two shared similar paths to show business. Both had grown up without affluence. Each attended a prestigious university and worked briefly in the corporate world. Price had gone to Stanford and had taken a position with an investment banking firm. Like Greg, she left her white-collar job after about a year.

"We always talked about how there's a difference between being very good at something and loving something that you're good at," said Price. "I think both of us had learned the lesson very early on."

Price landed the role. And production for the show's pilot episode began.

Greg's close friends and immediate family members went to Los Angeles for the *Common Law* pilot. Dave Chappelle also showed up to share the occasion. Filming a pilot did not mean the network would air the series, however. Greg waited with nervous excitement to hear the fate of *Common Law*.

"Every year there is a pilot that comes out of nowhere and gets picked up," said Gary Levine, a president at Witt/Thomas. "That's you guys this year."

ABC greenlit *Common Law*. Greg was beside himself. He called Steve Klein to share the news. He had little time to savor the moment. The next day he was picked up by a limo and met with Michael J. Fox, Brett Butler, Ellen DeGeneres, and other ABC stars. "The whole thing was surreal," said Klein.

Within 24 hours, Greg went from performing at a comedy club to being the face of a highly anticipated new sitcom. Greg attended ABC's upfronts at a posh amphitheater in New York. The upfronts are a live showcase for the television industry. The networks announce their fall schedules and try to entice media buyers with show excerpts, musical numbers, celebrity appearances, and other tactics. This event also marked the first time Greg saw edited clips of the show.

ABC promoted *Common Law* heavily. Greg had high hopes for it. He was featured in national advertisements. "There was a poster of him," said Dave Diamond. "He wore a purple suit . . . He was very excited." Robert Kurson, Greg's law school colleague, said that Greg "was blown away when he went into McDonald's and there was a placemat on the tray, promoting the show, and how it was stunning to him that we had just been in law school, whatever number of years ago, and now he was looking at himself on a tray in McDonald's."

People magazine included Greg on its list of "TV's most fascinating people."

The excitement continued as ABC sent Greg and Price along with Drew Carey and Shelley Fabares (from the network's two popular sitcoms, *The Drew Carey Show* and *Coach*) on a press tour.

The junket spanned the whole country—from New York to Dallas to the Raleigh-Durham area and all over the South. The actors flew from city to city and were greeted by mayors and representatives from local ABC stations. They attended expensive dinners and celebrated at lavish parties. They gave talks, shook hands, and mingled with guests to promote their shows.

Keeping true to his class-clown roots, Greg devised methods to amuse his friends—even at these celebrity get-togethers. Not one to take the Hollywood scene too seriously, Greg found his own ways to enjoy the ABC parties. He came up with a plan.

"I have this great idea, so just go with it," Greg said to Price.

Instead of discussing *Common Law*, Greg wanted to try his own version of crowd work. When meeting an executive or actor, he would purposely mistake the person for a more famous celebrity.

"Oh, it's an honor to meet you, Mr. Seinfeld," Greg remarked to a confused actor who looked almost nothing like the famous comedian. "I love your work."

Greg continued with the act and Price played along—changing the celebrity names as he worked the room. Maybe the guests were surprised. Perhaps they were too polite to interrupt. Either way, they rarely corrected him. The network may have disliked Greg's stunt, but it made his friend laugh. And that was enough for him.

Greg and Price had no prior experience with Hollywood publicity tours. While they found the travel grueling, they enjoyed the wining, dining, and limo rides. By the last day, however, all the actors were wiped out. The coffee and aspirin they had taken didn't help. Fabares passed out in the front seat of the limo on the way to the airport. "We get to the airport, we're all exhausted, we can't see straight," Price said—and then the kicker. She and Greg were crammed into the worst seats on plane. It was a bench at the back of the aircraft with no recliner option and right next to the lavatory.

"Well, I guess this is the glamour of Hollywood," Greg said.

Common Law premiered on Saturday, September 28, 1996, at 9:30 p.m. It had a strong lead-in from *Coach*, a highly rated show going into its eighth season. The competition at 9:30 came from *Early Edition* on CBS, *Love and Marriage* on Fox, and *The Pretender* on NBC. Greg was elated after the first episode. He bear-hugged Dorfman and said repeatedly, "Can you believe this is happening?"

During the premiere episode of *Common Law*, the Pope visits New York and Greg's character (John Alvarez) and his girlfriend (Nancy Slaton) are assigned an important case. Nancy focuses on getting the job done while John tries to bail an old friend out of jail.

In spite of Greg's and others' criticisms of his acting ability, the quality of the acting on *Common Law* was consistent with other sitcoms of the era. The writing, while not always cutting-edge, had some brilliant moments. However, certain aspects of the pilot episode likely wouldn't make it on a 21st-century sitcom. For example, during an exchange between John and his father about John's earring, the father says that jewelry is for "queers."

There are some memorable exchanges between John and the receptionist Maria (played by Diana Maria Riva):

> **John:** *Maria, why would Hector [her boyfriend] want to kill me?*
> **Maria:** *'Cause I'm always bragging that I work for this regular kid from Queens just like him. Except you went to Harvard Law School and you're gonna run this firm, and he went to reform school and scrubs urinals at Yankee Stadium.*

And between John and his boss, Martin (played by Richard Fancy):

> **Martin:** *You know, I'm not a particularly emotional man. Aside from dogs and cigars, very little gets me excited these days.*
> **John:** *There is a club in the Village you would love.*

Greg's look differed significantly from what it became in the 2000s. He was muscular with long hair and a thin beard. His character wore wide, brightly colored ties and dressed in office attire.

Future episodes were each based around a legal incident that required a resolution. John and a colleague win an important case against a large oil company, but one of John's comments to the media is misconstrued as a criticism of his Latino heritage. John's father, a barber, gets sued for refusing to cut a woman's hair. John takes the case of one of his heroes, a '60s radical.

Some of the writing is witty but lacks the hardcore intensity of Greg's standup. The show was a network sitcom after all—but many clever lines peep through:

> **Nancy:** *No, no, no, you tell me now and every relationship is irrevocably ruined. You me me him him you.*
> **John:** *I know someone who went to that school. Hawaii, right?*

Or John conceding just how little Nancy's parents think of him:

> **John:** *Your father hates me.*
> **Nancy:** *Well, I'm pretty sure my mother doesn't completely mind you.*
> **John:** *I feel that way about peas.*

Other characters also received some pretty memorable lines:

> **Nancy:** *You were dissatisfied with your eyebrow wax?*
> **Nancy's mother:** *One of them was higher than the other. I looked too quizzical.*

49

Greg's lack of theatrical training created some problems on set. "He had zero acting experience," said Rob LaZebnik, who created, wrote, and produced the show. "I don't think he even had been in junior high school plays. So this huge task was set in front of him and he hadn't even been doing standup for that long." Steve Klein said that Greg "never really mastered that acting thing" and Greg called himself a "terrible actor." Comedian Greg Fitzsimmons said, "He and I took acting classes together and I don't think either one of us felt like we really knew how to act our way out of a wet paper bag."

His inexperience showed. He would fail to be in the right position on stage and didn't always know how to look at the camera. LaZebnik said: "It's just an unbelievably daunting task . . . [he was] learning on the job in front of 300 people. It was really hard. I thought he actually did great. He was super appealing." Greg didn't play to the camera. "He always wanted the audience to have a good time," Price said. "If the audience wasn't laughing, then Greg wanted to change the joke."

LaZebnik relied on Price to carry the story lines to keep the audience engaged. Greg was there to be funny.

Greg was a generous actor and his performances improved over time. He didn't complain if his co-stars had more dialogue than he did. "Greg was not a line counter and was delighted to sit back and admire someone else's work," said LaZebnik.

"Often standups in that first season will freak out because it's super intense and scary and it's very foreign to what they're used to doing, but he was just the opposite. He was naturally very nervous during the pilot and maybe the first couple episodes, but he really settled into it quickly."

Greg displayed impressive acting skills on occasion—especially in scenes with Gregory Sierra, where he dropped his standup comedy instincts. He and Sierra took on a natural father–son dynamic. Greg didn't try to be funny. It didn't seem like acting at all. Price said that Greg became a true actor during his interactions with Sierra. "I think that [Sierra] felt like Greg's dad to him," said Price.

Two Comedians and Their Big Breaks

There's a curious intersection of two comedy careers involving the Montreal Comedy Festival and new sitcoms on ABC: Greg wasn't the only comedian who made a splash in Montreal and ended up with his own series on network television that year. So did Ray Romano, with *Everybody Loves Raymond*.

In fact, the first episodes of both shows were shot on the same day and in the same lot at Sunset Gower Studios in Hollywood. Greg and Megyn Price often hung out with Romano, as well as two of the cast members from *NewsRadio*, Dave Foley and

Maura Tierney. Greg and Romano also talked to each other about their experiences. Romano often said that he didn't know how to do this sitcom thing, but his approach was to make the show as real as possible. Greg, on the other hand, was playing a role that was not him: it was just a vehicle for jokes. Greg later reported his experiences to a friend, who told the story:

> Greg and Ray would commiserate after tapings, and he said that Ray always was like, "I don't know about this show." Greg was pretty confident in his, but it's also because Greg was pretty green. So Greg was like, "Ah, this is my big shot." Greg was on the cover of fuckin' TV Guide and shit that week, stuff like that. He was one of like the 50 beautiful people that year, in the fuckin' People magazine.

Everybody Loves Raymond premiered 15 days before Common Law and aired for nine seasons.

Several critics panned Common Law. David Bianculli of the New York Daily News called the show "unexceptional" and cited the main problem as the fact that the lines from Greg's standup routines did not translate well to a sitcom format. Others enjoyed it somewhat. John J. O'Connor in the New York Times praised Greg as "a talented stand-up comedian," but called the concept of the show "tired."

The show did not last. Before shooting began for the 13th episode, Tony Thomas of Witt/Thomas called the cast together to make an announcement.

"I have some news," said Thomas. "The show is canceled."

Before Greg and the others could digest what was said, Thomas continued: "But we're going to shoot the show tonight so that we will have 13 episodes we can sell, if possible, to the international market or to other people."

Greg turned to Price and whispered, "That's the worst pep talk I've ever heard." She laughed, as Greg said, "You're canceled. Now go be funny so we can maybe make some money."

ABC aired only four episodes of *Common Law* — the last one on October 19, 1996.

Some of those close to Greg claim that the cancellation wounded his psyche. They point to the show's demise as the reason Greg largely avoided referencing his legal background in the future.

A friend of Greg's said: "I feel like that really hurt his feelings. It was a nail in the coffin on his lawyer persona."

But LaZebnik disagreed, saying that although it was "hugely upsetting to be canceled," Greg didn't consider it an indictment — just a "series of events that led to not having an audience."

Dave Diamond said that Greg was sensitive about the show's cancellation for some time. He remembered an incident at the ABC building in New York a couple of years later: "It was raining in Manhattan and we went into . . . an ABC store in the lobby in New York and the guy actually said to us, 'Hey, do you guys like action figures? . . . We have memorabilia from a lot of ABC shows if you want to look around,' and I said to him, 'Well, do you have any action figures from *Common Law*?' I think it's really funny, but Greg was not happy at all . . . He was like, 'Fuck you, that's the meanest thing you could say to me.'"

Opinions vary on what caused *Common Law*'s cancellation. LaZebnik and Price partly blamed the time slot. Klein attributed it to "terrible" scripts, Greg's poor acting, and the fact that it didn't reflect Greg's sensibility. Klein said, "It was supposed to loosely be based on his life and they would — they said he's sort of the Hawkeye Pierce of the law, was sort of how they sort of pitched it because he had a guitar in his office and, he was the cool sort of unconventional, not afraid of putting it to the establishment guy. But we both sort of knew it wasn't great."

Price thought that the cancellation had nothing to do with Greg's performance. "Nobody was watching it to see the magical acting stylings of Greg Giraldo," said Price. "They were watching it to laugh. It was a show that had just gotten started and that needed some time to develop and to attract an audience." She also blamed the complexity and unpredictability of television, where there was "no rhyme or reason" and "so many corporations and personalities involved."

Greg's own assessment was in line with Price's. "These shows always suck at first," said Greg. "There was a lot of promise in the show — there were some great, really funny actors on the show — but ultimately it was pretty much dead right away. I mean, they put us on Saturday after *Coach*. *Coach* — which had been ABC's third-highest-rated show the year before — died that year. And in fact, after that, they abandoned programming on Saturday nights."

Disney's acquisition of ABC may have marked the end of *Common Law*. Greg said: "Jamie Tarses and all these people came in and other people left, so the people who had been in charge of the development process were replaced by other people who had no vested interest in the show. And they had an idea of what they wanted to do with the show, and they really wanted to sort of 'Spanish it up.' So it sort of became three separate shows going on all at once, and it was impossible to get anything done. I hadn't really been exposed to that scene out there enough to know how to fix it or fight it, and I was too busy trying to figure out what 'Stage Left' meant to kind of have any input into the creative side of it."

Greg characterized "Spanish it up" as "a million examples of just fucking horrific retardation." He mentioned that certain plot lines played off the worst kind of stereotypes. He shared an example of one involving a pregnancy scare with his girlfriend. "I guess they thought that she could be all stiff-upper-lippy and WASPy about it," said Greg. "And I would be all proud Latino, like, 'I banged that bitch and I knocked her up!'"

In a *People* magazine interview, Greg talked about the challenges of representing a culture. "Because I grew up in an Irish neighborhood, I never really identified myself with my ethnicity," said Greg, who didn't want to be viewed as "the torchbearer for all things Hispanic" just because he was on TV.

The fact that Greg's parents were Columbian and Spanish meant to some that he could represent Mexicans, Puerto Ricans, Cubans—effectively all Latin cultures. This disturbed Greg. He never relied on his background to develop a following. Many of his fans appreciated this. One said: "As an American-born Hispanic male, Greg Giraldo was a beacon of pride to a lot of us . . . He never once denied his Latin background but he never let it define him; he let his humanity do that."

Off camera Greg joked with Sierra about the network's desire to make an ethnic statement: "What, do you want us to wear sombreros and walk around eating tacos?"

Greg made it clear that he would reference his heritage, but didn't want to be a Hispanic spokesman. He was disappointed when some of the show's reviews focused on his ethnicity. Greg told Steve Weinstein in a *Los Angeles Times* interview:

> *It undermines your accomplishment . . . Instead of saying, "Great, we like the show," or even, "We don't think it's at all funny," it automatically became this suspicious thing. "Why are you on the air? Is it because you are Hispanic? It's because of the pressure put on ABC, isn't it?" . . . What I love about the show is that we're breaking stereotypes. There are Latino people of every shape and size and occupation and socioeconomic background, and that kind of speaks for itself. I'm proud that I can show that a guy like this, like me, does exist in this country, but it seems self-defeating to have to make such a big deal about it.*

And so Greg went back to what he did best—standup comedy. To many, standup was simply a springboard to television. Greg was the opposite. Although he had his own network sitcom, he didn't view standup as a road to something else. In fact, he worried that shooting a television show might compromise his ability to connect with live audiences. He never wanted TV to ruin that.

Greg still had standup, but he lost his agent. He told Jim Gaffigan that his agent dropped him after the show didn't work out. Soon after *Common Law*'s cancellation, Greg said that he saw his former agent dining at a restaurant. She acted like she didn't know him. "That's some fucking dark shit," said Gaffigan.

The grind of *Common Law* and disappointment at its abrupt ending weighed on Greg. Producers considered him a dream to work with, and with his favorable reputation, he likely would have landed another television spot—possibly as a late-night talk show host—but Greg missed the East Coast. So he flew home to New York.

Chapter 4
Marriage and Family

Special thanks to . . . most especially my three miraculous angelic demonic little Creeps, and mostest especialliest — my long suffering babies' momma, the greatest woman alive.

— Greg Giraldo

Back at home in New York, Greg focused on standup. He would write new jokes, refine old material, and get on stage almost nightly. One of the clubs where he fine-tuned his performances was Carolines. The club had been established by Caroline Hirsch in Chelsea in 1982, and she focused on "long sets for talent that was breaking through on television" rather than the typical short sets for new comedians who were trying to make it in the business. It worked. *Caroline's Comedy Hour* on A&E, a weekly show featuring some of the club's comedians, debuted in 1989 and lasted for five seasons. The club's success ultimately led to its move to Times Square in 1992. With 300 seats and 100 more at the bar, the new location was a large and fancy venue and less gritty than many of the other comedy clubs that Greg would ultimately perform at.

It was at Carolines that Greg noticed a gorgeous dark-haired woman serving drinks to patrons. MaryAnn McAlpin, a costume designer, worked in the cue card department at *Saturday Night Live* and moonlighted part-time as a waitress at Carolines. She caught Greg's attention. Several female comedy club employees appreciated Greg's charm and good looks. In fact, it became a running joke with some of Greg's comedian friends. However, he never dated any of the women from the clubs—until he met MaryAnn.

She didn't normally date any of the comics she met. But Greg was different. Greg and MaryAnn discussed their Latin backgrounds and love of travel. She had just moved back to New York City after a stint in Spain, where she worked at the 1992 Barcelona Olympic Games. She missed Spain and was saddled with debt after taking a trip around the world. Greg mentioned that his mother was from Granada, Spain, and he shared with MaryAnn that he spent summers in Spain. A friendship began.

Greg eventually noticed an attraction and confided to Jim Gaffigan: "I think that waitress MaryAnn likes me."

But Gaffigan wasn't encouraging. He said, "MaryAnn is beautiful. These waitresses at Carolines looked like they were from music videos . . . I'm like, 'You're drunk. There's no way that that girl likes *you*.'"

By 1994, after about six months, the friendship had developed into a romantic relationship. Mary-Ann said: "We went from hanging out a couple times to almost being inseparable. And then we were like that for years. He didn't even move in. He was actually staying at a friend's hotel space. He wasn't renting a room. He was over my place all the time . . . We were together all the time. We would go to the gym together and come home together. I would go on the road with him."

Greg's friends noticed how close they were as a couple. MaryAnn not only supported Greg's comedy goals, but she also provided more balance to his life. They laughed often and took frequent trips to the park. Diamond saw them together many times and would occasionally meet up with them at Central Park: "I was on the East Side and they lived on the West Side and we'd meet at the park. Mary-Ann would bring a blanket and food sometimes, or we would just walk around and get chicken wings on the West Side." Estee Adoram, the booker at the Comedy Cellar, remembered a dinner out with the two of them: "They were walking ahead . . . holding each other, and it was a very nice night. It was almost like a picture type of thing."

As Greg and MaryAnn's relationship grew, Greg met more of her family. In 1995, her relatives organized a family reunion in New York City. A couple of days before the picnic, she invited her cousin Erik Lievano, who had yet to meet Greg, to a show at Carolines to watch Greg perform.

Greg went on stage at 9 p.m., but Lievano missed the R train from Brooklyn to Manhattan, making him 15 minutes late to the show.

Once Lievano arrived at Carolines, the stage was bright but the seating area was dim. Lievano navigated stealthily through the audience hoping to avoid getting noticed. He thought to himself, *I don't want to be targeted as "that guy" by any of the comics — the guy that strolls in late and looks like an asshole for missing half the gig.*

He was nearly in the clear, but he wasn't so lucky. Greg — about a quarter of the way through his 40-minute set — noticed someone rustling among the showgoers. Just before Lievano sat down, Greg unleashed one of his classic insult barrages.

"Look at this jerkoff, strolling in late and fucking up my gig," Greg announced. "What happened, dude? Did you oversleep? Holy shit, man, you're killing me."

Suddenly the spotlight went right on Lievano, and the crowd erupted in laughter. Mortified, Lievano remained seated while his face turned red.

After the show, MaryAnn formally introduced Greg to Lievano and a befuddled Greg said, "Dude, I'm so sorry. I didn't realize that you were Mary-Ann's cousin Erik. I thought you were just some random guy walking in late." Greg went on, "If I had known, I would never have targeted you like that."

Lievano replied, "It's all good. I would have done the same thing to someone if I had the chance."

The next day Lievano experienced a side of Greg unavailable to most of Greg's fans. Greg met him in Manhattan to deliver a large bag of bagels for the family picnic that Lievano was to take to his father's house in Brooklyn. Greg and MaryAnn drove Lievano to his subway stop in lower Manhattan.

Throughout the car ride, Greg asked him continually if he was going to be all right, inquiring if he knew the right train to catch. Greg didn't relent.

"Are you sure you're going to be all right by yourself taking the train?" Greg asked.

Lievano's brother had died in a subway accident just one year before this reunion. He reassured Greg several times that he was fine and then hopped out of their car with the enormous bag of bagels in hand and headed down the stairs toward the subway platform. Lievano sat for about three minutes on the subway bench waiting for his train. Suddenly, Greg ran down the concrete steps to meet him.

"I can't let you catch the subway all alone with a bag of food," Greg implored. "Let me drive you back to Brooklyn."

"Why?" Lievano asked.

Greg sheepishly responded, "I don't know, man—just everything that happened—please let me drive you to Brooklyn."

He accepted Greg's offer and the two walked back up the stairs to street level where Greg's car was double-parked with MaryAnn waiting patiently in the passenger seat. The three of them enjoyed the

30-minute ride to hand-deliver the bagels. Greg and Lievano built a lasting friendship.

As Greg and MaryAnn fell more deeply in love, they spent less time apart. Greg warmed to the idea of getting married again. He wanted to make it official. MaryAnn accepted Greg's marriage proposal. He moved into her rent-controlled apartment, and the wedding planning began.

Greg wanted to look dapper for the big day. And his hair played a big part in this.

Greg complained that his hair was too thick and that nothing could be done with it. So he called in a favor and got connected to Salvador, a celebrity stylist who went by his first name only and cut George Clooney's hair. Greg and Salvador got along well, but maybe not to the extent that Greg imagined. He passed on a friend's offer to pay for his wedding haircut, assuming Salvador would give him a break on the price. Salvador did cut Greg's hair. It looked great. But it cost him $500. While Greg tended to his hair, MaryAnn applied her decorating talents to transform a city bar into a chic marriage venue.

The bride and groom enjoyed a beautiful but nontraditional New York City wedding on January 23, 1999, a date Greg later had tattooed on his biceps. "It was in a small bar in Manhattan, and it was awesome," said Matt Paroly, who attended both of Greg's weddings. A 20-piece funk-style band from Café Wha?, a music club located steps from the Comedy Cellar, entertained the guests. A trio of lead singers made sporadic announcements throughout the celebration. "When Greg first walked in," announced a female singer, "I said to myself, 'That boy is gorgeous.'"

The event had a classy, metropolitan feel to it, and it was a much different affair from Greg's first marriage ceremony. Now 33 years old, Greg celebrated with his comedy buddies and family members. Comedian Dave Attell made a hilariously off-color speech that would have gotten him thrown out of most weddings. "We were laughing so hard. It was so inappropriate," a guest said. Not the least bit offended, the crowd enjoyed Attell's irreverent homage to Greg and MaryAnn.

Later that year, the newlyweds packed their bags for a six-week honeymoon. Growing up, Greg traveled frequently and typically flew standby — a perk of his father's for working at an airline. However, he grew tired of the uncertainty of standby. As a gift to themselves, he and MaryAnn booked assigned-seat tickets to Southeast Asia. They first stayed in Hong Kong and then Bali. For the more adventurous portion of their retreat, Greg and MaryAnn backpacked through Thailand and Vietnam. They took in some of the most picturesque sights on the planet. "It was amazing. It was so spectacular," MaryAnn said of their arrival on the Phi Phi Islands in Thailand. This chain of six islands would become a tourist hotbed a year later, with the release of the Leonardo DiCaprio film, *The Beach*. In the meantime, this beach resort served as an uncrowded paradise to scuba divers and fortunate travelers. "There's no way we're leaving," Greg said to his new bride after seeing the limestone cliffs and turquoise water. MaryAnn, a certified scuba diver, helped Greg get certified during their trip. They had planned on staying in Thailand for only a few days, but the scenic beaches and $12 per night lodging costs motivated them to extend their stay for another week.

That fall Greg and MaryAnn took another significant step. They bought their first home together—they had some money saved from MaryAnn's inheritance and Greg's work on *Common Law*. Looking back, MaryAnn said: "I definitely pushed him to buy our first apartment. He was very stressed about it . . . His reaction was, 'Are you calling me from the unemployment line telling me that we have an accepted offer?'"

MaryAnn had a knack for renovating real estate —she could help add value to their investment, but Greg still had some reluctance about making such a significant purchase. They moved forward—each contributing half of the down payment for the 1,100-square-foot unit. Greg and MaryAnn were now struggling artists and Manhattan real estate owners.

Their first place as homeowners was a significant step up from the rented studio apartment. When Greg and MaryAnn settled in, the apartment was a formal one bedroom—it had a dining room, a living room, and a bedroom. MaryAnn's design skills were again put to good use. She helped convert the dining room into a living room and added a second bedroom.

The spare room didn't stay vacant for long. They welcomed their first son in 2000. Greg, an excited new dad, wasted little time in sharing the good news. He went to a nearby comedy club where one of his friends asked about the name of Greg's baby.

"Gregory Carlos Giraldo, Jr.," Greg replied clearly and deliberately, enunciating each word of his son's name.

Parenthood brings less sleep, more responsibility, and constant adjustments for any couple. Greg and MaryAnn dealt with this, too, but also enjoyed the excitement of building their own family. MaryAnn said that in spite of some of the hardships, "I look back at those times and we were so happy. We were so in love with Gregory."

Greg and MaryAnn had two more sons: Daniel in 2003 and Lucas in 2004. Greg reveled in each birth. He loved his boys—a fact that friends and family acknowledged and that he himself said many times in interviews. Greg "was amazing with his kids and with kids in general," Steve Klein said. "He was very cool with my kids. He was a fun guy and had no trouble bringing the level down to five years of age and that sort of thing." Megyn Price added:

"I've never seen anything like it in my life, how much he loved his kids."

When MaryAnn was pregnant with their third child, she had a toddler, an eight-month-old, and a job. She needed rest and wanted more space for the family. Her handiwork on their apartment had paid off. The property had doubled in value.

Greg lobbied to move to the suburbs, but Mary-Ann found a lovely 1,600-square-foot apartment on the Upper West Side south of Columbia University. It was a "classic six" — meaning it had three bath-rooms, two bedrooms, and a maid's quarters, in ad-dition to great light and Central Park views. The apartment needed work, but MaryAnn was up to the challenge. Greg required more convincing.

During the final walk-through with their real estate agent, Greg said to MaryAnn, "Wow, you've been really lucky so far, but this time if you fuck up we're ruined."

They closed escrow, and MaryAnn went to work refinishing floors and painting the walls. Greg was impressed with the changes MaryAnn made, saying "maybe you're on to something." Greg now had his own home office and MaryAnn had some space to herself. During this time, Greg's schedule picked up, with regular appearances on a fledgling new Come-dy Central show called *Tough Crowd with Colin Quinn* and a more intense touring calendar. In spite of the busier schedule, Greg and MaryAnn made family a priority.

Greg enjoyed taking his sons out for ice cream. His sense of humor came through on these outings. On occasion, Greg would lick the ice cream before handing it over to his kids. He would say: "It's a taste tax. That's my cut."

As Greg made more money, his hobbies got more expensive. Boating became a passion. He purchased a boat, which he housed in Brooklyn. Boating allowed Greg to relax with his family and calm his busy mind. He felt more present on the water and loved the experience.

This passion did not translate to expertise. "Greg was a terrible boat captain," said a friend who boated with him. "You typically found yourself in the post–9/11 protected waters off of JFK and being boarded by the Coast Guard or being stuck on a sandbar in shallow water and boarded by the Coast Guard. Thankfully, even the Coast Guard loved Greg."

Comedian Tom Papa once joined Greg for a boating trip. Papa recalled that Greg was grateful that comedy had helped bring them to the point where they could afford to spend a day on the water. Greg suggested that they try to sail around Manhattan. Neither of them had done this before. When they hit the northern tip of the island, they noticed a small hut that looked like a tollbooth.

They thought they would have to circle back to the starting point. Then the gates opened and a friendly attendant waved them through. Greg and Tom Papa successfully circled Manhattan.

"For that little brief moment there, we were just really, really enjoying life," Papa said.

For several years, Greg served as a role model for comics who wanted to have a happy home life. Comedian Tom Shillue, who as a single man in the 1990s grappled with the idea of getting married, said that Greg had contributed to his change of attitude. "I remember getting out at the Strip and be like 'Hey, do you want to go shoot pool?' He's like, 'Nah, I got to go home.' It's like, 'Oh, Giraldo's going home.' I remember thinking, *OK, he's got his act together here. We're still idiots.*"

Shillue warmed to the idea of marriage and would eventually cite Greg as an example of someone who made it work. He said: "Now I tell comics that all the time, these unmarried guys, I'm like, 'Just get married. Just shut up and do it, you dummy,' and I thought that Giraldo had solved that early on." Shillue admired Greg's commitment to MaryAnn and their family: "I remember being at Gaffigan's wedding and Giraldo was there with his wife and I remember she was just so cute and I just thought, *Oh, look at those two.*"

Greg's ability to maintain a home life without losing his comedic edginess impressed several comics, including Robert Kelly, who often performed with Greg in New York City.

Kelly was inspired by Greg. He realized that he could be a father and husband and still be funny. "You don't have to be out there using drugs and banging chicks without condoms to fucking have an edge," said Kelly.

Some of Greg's close friends noticed no major change in him when he became a father, just that he had "extra chores" to do. He managed the situation practically, spending most of his time with his children in the early part of the week and then working at clubs most Thursdays through Sundays. Greg would regularly call home to chat with MaryAnn and his sons.

Being away from his loved ones took a toll on Greg. He wanted to provide for them, but he also missed them terribly.

The unpredictability of Greg's travel schedule added more stress for him and MaryAnn. After a show at Zanies in St. Charles, Illinois, Greg called MaryAnn to notify her that he would be on the road longer than planned. The news frustrated both of them, and Greg vented his feelings to the audience.

Greg remarked, "All couples fight. We've all had the same fights. You know exactly the ones I'm talking about."

The crowd related to Greg's premise, and then he took a sharp turn: "You know the one when you're bombing at an empty club in Wheeling, West Virginia, and some toothless douche in the front row is like, 'You ain't from around here, are ya, boy?'"

Greg then asked, "Did you really just say that, you clichéd, slobbering, mongoloid half-wit? People still say inbred, cracker-ass shit like that?"

In a cartoonish hillbilly accent, Greg answered, "Man, you suck. You ain't funny at all."

"Then you're like, 'Don't get mad at me cuz you caught your rattail in the Tilt-A-Whirl at work today, fuckface."

At this point, the crowd broke out in laughter. Greg continued: "I didn't tell you to drop out of high school and eat rock candy 15 hours a day for the last 15 years. I'm pretty sure you came up with that approach to life all by your own inbred, cousin-fucking self."

Reverting back to the hillbilly character, Greg said, "'Man, I'm gonna kick your ass.' Then I'm like, 'Why don't you kick my ass then, motherfucker?' So you get off stage and start doing shots of tequila just to numb the pain. Then you're on the phone with your wife, and she's like, 'Are you drunk?'

"'Yeah, I'm drunk. I'm in West Virginia. I'm gonna stay drunk the whole goddamned time I'm here.'"

Quickly, Greg changed his voice to a higher sound and added, "'Well, I hate going on the road too, my love, but I'm just trying to earn a god-damned living here, okay?'"

Greg expressed his frustrations about the road, relationships, expectations for a minute or so, and concluded the bit by saying: "You take what you originally found attractive and appealing about a person and mash them into a neutered little puppy dog, which is subconsciously what you originally wanted in the first place." The joke concluded with Greg asking the audience, "Have you had that one a lot? It's the same shit, right?"

The stage provided a cathartic outlet for Greg. But when he returned home, he had to address the same issues that impact most families. Around 2005, Greg and MaryAnn decided to take their children out of an expensive private school and enroll them in one of the city's best public schools. This helped lower their bills, but it didn't eliminate Greg's anxiety. MaryAnn herself saw it build as their family grew:

> *Every time I got pregnant I think he would get so nervous. He would say, "It's almost an animalistic instinct of, 'Oh, my God, I need to provide.'" So he would go on the road more. In retrospect, I'm sure he was scared. It's scary, daunting being a parent, and knowing for him this is his Latin roots thinking,* Oh, my God, I have to provide for them. *So I think that did drive him and actually worked in his favor because it pushed him to other limits. It is true that with every kid he got more and more successful.*

Greg wanted to replicate the type of stable home life that his parents gave him, but he faced personal issues that made it more difficult to achieve. He couldn't escape his feelings of inadequacy. Perhaps it emanated from some type of depression, but Greg's mental distress impacted his family. It also caused him to seek remedies to treat his angst. Alcohol gave him a temporary reprieve. Comedian Greg Fitzsimmons said that Greg tried desperately to be a good family man, but that drinking made it difficult. "There's a lot of lying to cover up that kind of living," said Fitzsimmons. "And you just can't have that in a marriage."

Comedian Judy Gold lived near Greg. They would often discuss parenting. Gold noticed that Greg seemed tortured inside and feared that he would succumb to his vices. She said: "It was so unbelievable because when you look at him, you'd see, 'You're so fucking talented. You went to Columbia and Harvard. You're so fucking smart.'" Gold wanted to shake Greg and yell at him: "Don't you see you have it all?"

Both Gold and Fitzsimmons alluded to Greg's drinking and drug use. It wasn't a new thing for MaryAnn. Very early in their relationship, she had seen signs of it. "I definitely have very clear memories of wanting to go home because I was working, and he just never wanted to go home. He always wanted to go out for one more drink," she said.

Greg may have turned to alcohol and drugs as a way to cope with his internal struggles, but the effects of his substance abuse impacted his focus and behavior as a father. He loved his children—"our kids always knew that we loved them, that was never in question," said MaryAnn—but his friend Joe Schrank reminded Greg that his addiction was having an effect on his children—and the children noticed it. "He had a lot of denial about his kids . . . I would say, 'Greg, you're full of shit. They know. If they don't know exactly what's going on, they know that something isn't right. It's got long-reaching ripple effects in your lives. You're out of your fucking mind if you think that this isn't affecting them,'" Schrank said.

Greg and MaryAnn entered couples therapy— this helped Greg come to terms with his addiction and see that it was a diagnosed illness. But there were major challenges to overcome. During a session, the therapist told them that there was no point in going to therapy until Greg treated his own condition.

"You can't go to therapy if you're an active addict," the therapist told Greg. "You're not even going to remember anything that we're saying."

This message hit home for Greg, who felt incredibly guilty about what his family had to endure. It gave MaryAnn comfort, knowing that he had heard it from a licensed professional. Greg worked to improve his health, but he struggled. MaryAnn, who had witnessed her own father's bouts with alcoholism, wanted desperately to help Greg. But she knew it was his battle to fight. She saw signs that were less obvious to others. She noticed that sometimes Greg's hands would shake, a symptom of alcohol withdrawal.

As Greg's drinking issues worsened, MaryAnn stepped up and worked feverishly to help maintain the relationship between her three sons and their father. The situation was serious. The family spent tens of thousands of dollars to send Greg to rehab. MaryAnn, however, thought about much more than just money. "All I want is for the kids to be able to spend time with him," she said. "Because I don't expect him to live."

Through all the tribulations, Greg's love for his children never wavered, and they provided delight to their father. Greg's friend, Tom Johnson, a writer for *The Daily Show*, remembered one of Greg's fondest moments: "One of his happiest times, though, was when he and his oldest son starred in an NYPD-style detective sketch on *Stand-Up Nation*. They played partner NYPD detectives. He loved that. He was never happier. Even sitting in his office with his son after the day of taping it, he was just glowing."

Unfortunately, Greg's addiction eroded their home life. It pained MaryAnn to see the man she loved suffer from a condition that was hurting more than just himself. She knew he might need to hit rock bottom before things improved.

Greg's unpredictability became too much to endure. His behavior grew so detrimental that mental health professionals advised MaryAnn to take a drastic step. In what was the toughest decision of her life, in 2008, she asked Greg to move out of the family home. Ultimately, MaryAnn had to focus on her children. She hoped that the separation would allow Greg to get the help he needed to better himself and improve their family dynamic. She felt for her husband. "I always loved him," MaryAnn said. "We were very close."

In the midst of his personal tussles, Greg's career accelerated. He played more clubs and earned greater acclaim for his comedy. As his fame rose, Greg performed with fewer boundaries. Greg and MaryAnn would talk on the phone frequently after his shows, and she helped rein in some of his more personal bits by appealing to Greg's strong sense of family.

Now 42 years old, Greg moved in with his good friend and sober companion, Joe Schrank. He and MaryAnn announced their separation. The Giraldos' home life stabilized somewhat.

"At that point, we didn't fight anymore," Mary-Ann said. "Once he accepted it was an illness, there was no point in me fighting about something he had no control over."

.

Chapter 5
A Comedian's Mind

The best comics are like the most beautiful strippers.
They're the most damaged.

– Joey Gay

In October 2004, Jay Dixit, a writer with the *New York Times*, received an interesting assignment. He had to tackle entry-level comedy. "I thought open mics were places for comedians to test out material," said Dixit. His perception changed after he attended a show on the Lower East Side. He watched hours of self-loathing and pain. He found several examples of comics who failed.

Failure is something that all comedians experience. They bomb on stage. A part that they auditioned for goes to someone else. They make a pilot for television, but the network doesn't pick it up.

Five years later, Dixit led a series on failure for the magazine *Psychology Today*.

Dixit wanted to interview a successful comedian. By 2009, Greg had been doing comedy professionally for almost 20 years. Audiences loved him and comedians respected him. From Dixit's perspective, Greg was the perfect counterpoint to failure. He connected with Greg. What transpired shocked him.

In his interview for *Psychology Today* in May of that year, Greg revealed that the outward success was not something he felt or saw in himself.

"I'm constantly tortured by a sense of failure," Greg told Dixit. "I feel like quitting all the time."

Dixit was surprised not only by Greg's perception of himself, but by the open, honest, and thoughtful way in which he spoke. In Dixit's long experience as a journalist, this was rare.

Several times, Greg referred to himself as a "fuckup" and criticized his perceived lack of resiliency. "I'm not a 'get knocked down and just pull myself back up by my bootstraps and come back harder' kind of guy," he said. He admitted to "this constant feeling of not having achieved enough . . . the sense that I suck constantly . . . frustrated with myself and my limitations."

Greg was not perfect, of course, and some of his harsh self-assessments were accurate. "I'm constantly tormented by the fact that if I could get organized enough to just sit down and write, I would be 50 times further than I am today, creatively," he said. During his time preparing for *Tough Crowd*, Greg excelled under the constraints of deadlines and deliverables, but in the less structured environment of a comedy tour, his creative output flagged. He also received regular requests from film executives asking him for movie ideas, but after coming up with some concepts, Greg said, "I get all fucking ADD and the opportunity slips away."

Apart from the ability to be a disciplined writer, though, Greg had many skills and accomplishments. Comedy clubs wanted him to headline. His peers admired his artistry. Television producers paid to work with him. Still, he criticized himself for falling short of his potential. High achievers such as Greg often hold themselves to unrealistic standards. In one sense, it helps them, it drives them, it pushes them past plateaus. But expectations can get so elevated that they create a constant sense of failure. Greg *looked* for examples of himself as a failure, and of course he found them. The cycle continued.

"It's confirmation bias," Dixit explained. "If you think you're a fuckup, you're going to find reasons to justify your belief."

Greg's issues with self-confidence became so severe that he wondered if he even deserved to be a comedian. "That was such an insane thing for a guy like that," said Colin Quinn. "A lot of young comedians looked up to him the most by far as the guy they loved." Greg worried about the effect of being perceived as unsuccessful, a "loser" whose projects never "take off." He didn't care about the lambasting he often got at the comedy roasts—he famously dished it out too—but he did worry that some people might conclude that the jibes about him were actually real.

"It's not so much the jokes, I just worry that it will become a self-fulfilling prophecy," Greg said. "Like, great, I'm Greg—the guy that kills fucking pilots. It maybe gets to me on that level. There's maybe this little part of me that thinks, *Fuck, maybe they're right. I haven't really accomplished anything they can make fun of."*

In conversations with friends, Greg discussed suffering from the impostor syndrome—an internal experience of intellectual phoniness that researchers say "interferes with the psychological well-being of a person." The consequences are very real, and those impacted confront fear, stress, self-doubt, and feel uncomfortable with their achievements. The results can be debilitating, and the more success the person has, the more they focus on how much they are below their ideal, "strengthening the feeling of being a fraud or an impostor."

This continuous self-flagellation can drive people deeper into depression. Certain comics believe that such suffering helps the creative process. Not Greg.

"Some people do better when they're in a bitter, angry place," Greg said to Dixit. "I don't. I think I'm funniest when I'm feeling more optimistic, hopeful about everything."

Other comedians are not so fortunate, partly due to the difficult path that they have to navigate to achieve even some semblance of success. "Comedy is fucking hard!" Dixit put it succinctly. In many careers, one can follow a preset path. Doctors attend medical school, train as a resident, and practice medicine. Lawyers graduate from law school, take the bar, and go to work in an office. They generally benefit from pay raises and job security.

It's different for comedians. They have to write their own jokes, define their persona, create on the fly as they try to find their place in a continuously changing industry. There is no final stage for standups. Dissatisfaction is the norm. "I know people who have played Madison Square Garden: they want to know why they're not movie stars," said comedian Natasha Leggero. "I think I know maybe two people who are satisfied with their careers . . . It's just an ongoing struggle for comedians, this idea of ambition and success."

What Greg Was vs. What He Thought About Himself

One result of Greg's misperception of himself as a failure and a fraud was how he reacted to the outward success of other comedians. His psyche, his highly developed brain, had difficulty processing the dichotomy of being a popular comedian versus being a more underground or niche comic. In his later days, Greg became a staunch admirer of comedian Doug Stanhope. He respected how Stanhope always said exactly whatever he wanted to. (Stanhope was also a fan of Greg, calling him "smarter and funnier than I'll ever be.")

Stanhope's comedy is not for all tastes, and he isn't well known outside of fairly narrow comic circles. On the other end of the spectrum is a comedian such as Dane Cook. Producer Joel Gallen said Cook "crushed" during the Insomniac Tour with Dave Attell, but also highlighted the differences between Greg's and Cook's styles.

Greg did "smart joke telling and [was] sophisticated, kind of unusual and off-the-beaten-path type." Cook, on the other hand, "knew how to market himself, and Dane probably had a great publicist. There was a method to his madness," but Greg "was more of an artist." He was the sharp satirist to Cook's slick populist.

Writing and performing mattered more to him. Publicity was an afterthought. He admired Stanhope and Lenny Bruce for their willingness to address dark topics and speak without inhibition. Like Greg, these comedians built cult followings but never totally broke through to the masses.

One irony was that even in the midst of constant self-doubt and an overriding sense of professional failure, Greg remained dedicated to the art of standup. Fellow comic Jay Mohr said that Greg "stayed true to comedy, and would not waver." His occasional impatience with some network executives was detrimental to his career in practical terms, but his frustration came from the respect he had for the craft of standup.

"He was very true to his comedy," Mohr said. "I wish personally, because he's not here anymore, that he was more truthful to himself."

Greg was not afraid to take risks on stage and he didn't always play it safe with his material. This helped Greg stand out comedically, but the risky material sometimes clashed with his natural empathy. He could be overly sensitive to those who felt alienated or offended by his edgier humor. Many comedians are able to separate the two aspects of their person more categorically. Patrice O'Neal, who famously sparred with him, was one of those. O'Neal could cut hard at any topic or even an audience member, and he always laughed it off and just moved on. It doesn't mean that he was heartless. He was just more able than Greg was to make the separation between what he was performing on stage and how it might affect the person he was talking about.

As an example, Greg and Schrank made a series of online videos, with one involving Greg interviewing a supplier of communion wafers used for the Eucharist in Catholic church services. Greg asked if the wafers came in different flavors, such as jalapeño for Latinos. This bit caused someone from his high school to send him an angry email. Greg took the criticism to heart. He worried that he had offended the entire Regis High community. He thought that they all hated him, which was not the case at all.

Many comics fight this battle between wanting to perform at their unfettered peak, but also being excessively self-critical. Jessica Kirson referred to the comedian as the "piece of shit in the center of the universe" — egotistical enough to want to be the focus of attention, but often with a very self-deprecatory mindset and leading a lonely and isolated life.

"It's all about ego," Kirson added. "It's all about being rejected. It's dark. It's scary. It's isolating." And it can lead to depression.

More than 10 percent of the population suffers from depression or anxiety, explained Lindsay Merrill, MD, a Harvard-trained psychiatrist. The stigma surrounding mental illness creates unique treatment challenges. Willpower alone will not cure depression. "I tell my patients, 'If you had diabetes, would you say, "Come on, just make more insulin"?'" said Dr. Merrill. "I would never say that. Well, it's the same with depression." She maintained that without treatment, those dealing with depression are often unable to turn off the mind chatter that tells them they're not good enough. Many comedians are prone to this kind of self-destructive internal script.

The overall result for Greg was that he was "never really at peace with himself," said Joe

Schrank. Never satisfied, always "restless, irritable, and discontented" in spite of his success. "I would say to him, 'I don't know. If being the son of immigrants and graduating from Harvard and being on Comedy Central doesn't convince you that you're doing all right, I have no words for you, Greg.'"

But it was also more serious than that, more ingrained and primal. Megyn Price, the co-star of *Common Law* and Greg's friend for 15 years, said that his biggest fault was that "he just didn't protect himself, ever." He had no trouble being himself on stage, but when those same walls were down in his personal life it caused him much pain. His openness made him vulnerable to getting hurt. He was concerned about others but he didn't always take care of himself. He lacked that balance.

"He wanted everyone around him to be happy," said his friend Tom Johnson. "Imagine the weight of that."

Yet despite it all—the whole messy business of being a comedian and the effect that it had on his relationships with others and his perception of himself—mainly, Greg recognized the positive in the crazy career he had chosen.

"I'm really proud of what I can do with standup comedy," Greg said. "I'm living the life I've always wanted, in a lot of ways."

Chapter 6
Tough Crowd

It was a bit menacing in its confrontational style of humor, but there's never been anything like it.
— Marc Maron

Days after the 9/11 terrorist attacks, Greg felt compelled to return to the stage. While still rattled by the tragedy, Greg chose to perform just miles away from where the World Trade Center had stood. Unsure of what he would say and how the crowd would respond, Greg left his Upper West Side apartment and boarded a nearly empty subway. The usual noise of busy commuters was absent on this night. Peering down the eerily quiet cabin, Greg noticed another passenger. Jim Gaffigan sat calmly on the same subway en route to Stand Up NY. Greg approached his friend and said, "We need to talk about this. This is our thing." Gaffigan responded, "I think it's also important for us not to talk about it, for us to have an escape from this anxiety."

Greg and Gaffigan, like millions of other Americans, could find little respite from the fear and unease that the attacks had caused. Figuring out what role comedy should play challenged even the most experienced comedians. The intersection of politics and comedy is difficult to navigate even in peaceful times. With terrorism and possible war dominating the national conversation, comedians faced a more formidable task in discussing divisive topics.

Although the best comedians use humor to help make sense of pain in the midst of tragedy, their attempts can also fall flat. Shortly after the 9/11 hijackings, comedian Bill Maher made a comment on his show *Politically Incorrect* that drew intense ire. In a discussion about whether the terrorists who flew the planes into the World Trade Center buildings were cowards, Maher said: "*We* have been the cowards, lobbing cruise missiles from 2,000 miles away—that's cowardly. Staying in the airplane when it hits the building—say what you want about it: not cowardly." These remarks caused controversy and ultimately got Maher fired. A couple of weeks later, comedian Gilbert Gottfried joked during his performance at the Friars Club roast of Hugh Hefner: "I have to leave early tonight. I have to fly out to L.A. I couldn't get a direct flight, I have to make a stop at the Empire State Building." The crowd gasped, booed, and shouted at Gottfried indignant cries of "too soon."

During this time, Greg deftly offered his first jokes about the attacks. In one bit, Greg mentioned seeing a bachelorette party after 9/11. Several of the women in the group wore rubber penises on their heads. "We're going to be okay," Greg said, alluding to the sentiment that the terrorists hadn't won. "Life goes on." In character, Greg mimicked an inebriated friend of the bachelorette who won't let "those Mexicans from al-Qaeda" ruin their big day—demonstrating the endurance of the American spirit.

Comedian Ted Alexandro watched Greg perform that joke and admired how Greg skillfully used humor to unite during such a sensitive time. "He was smart enough to make the smart joke but broad enough to cast a wide net," Alexandro remarked. "Like everyone was in on the joke."

A year later, the initial shock of 9/11 had somewhat subsided. The landscape of humor began to reshape itself. Audiences reacted less harshly to material critical of America. Comedians tackled more issues of global policy. Stewart, as host of *The Daily Show*, became the de facto leader of the country's burgeoning comedy infotainment renaissance. He conducted a dialogue—melding comedy with politics—that resonated with many. By late 2002, Stewart was a pop-culture fixture and regarded highly by critics—winning the Emmy Award for Outstanding Variety Series every year from 2003 to 2012.

Tough Crowd with Colin Quinn debuted on December 9, 2002, but the origins of the talk show were more than a decade earlier. On almost any night during the 1990s and early 2000s, arguments broke out among comedians at the Olive Tree Café and Bar above the Comedy Cellar. These verbal clashes involved anything from religion, race, and politics, to Christina Aguilera's music, the New York Yankees' dominance, and Jim Norton's appearance.

Greg thrived in this environment. One of Greg's sparring partners, Tom Shillue, recalled certain insights he gleaned from these late-evening squabbles: "Greg could crush you with his knowledge. He wasn't a bleeding-heart type of guy, but he did understand frailty . . . It was almost like intellectual jousting, and he would flatten me sometimes."

Quinn, who frequently joined the discussions at the table, had a revelation. As the world seemed to become more politically correct, Comedy Cellar comedians talked more candidly on stage about taboo subjects. Comics embraced the challenge. Quinn noticed that the crowd was not bothered by this bold, raw approach to standup. They laughed harder. This observation inspired Quinn to create his own television show based on the honest and unrestrained debates above the Comedy Cellar.

In early 2002, just two years after leaving *Saturday Night Live*, Quinn reunited with Lorne Michaels, the famed *SNL* producer, to collaborate on a new development. They created *The Colin Quinn Show* — the forerunner of *Tough Crowd*.

Filmed live on the same stage where Quinn had hosted *SNL's* "Weekend Update," the first incarnation ran from March 11 until March 25, 2002. The production included a monologue, sketches, and a town hall segment where comedians debated preset topics. "It wasn't like *Tough Crowd*, where you didn't dare rehearse a bit," said Jim Norton, who appeared on the first episode of *The Colin Quinn Show* with Comedy Cellar regulars Patrice O'Neal, Nick Di Paolo, and Keith Robinson. "This was like we were actually doing a one-minute bit each about a subject." Celebrity guests, including Cheri Oteri and Rosie O'Donnell, joined Quinn to boost the show's marketability. The series differed from most major-network comedy shows in that it addressed grave issues such as bomb threats, anthrax scares, and racial profiling in a brutally honest format. "You gotta give Lorne Michaels credit for taking a chance," said Di Paolo. NBC pulled the plug on *The Colin Quinn Show* after three episodes.

About nine months later, Comedy Central offered a more appropriate home for Quinn's original idea. This next iteration, *Tough Crowd with Colin Quinn*, borrowed the framework of its NBC predecessor. As host, Quinn kicked off each episode with an opening monologue before leading a collection of four comedians through "four rounds of smart comedy" that included lively discussions and planned segments. Comedy Central ran eight test episodes in November 2002. *Tough Crowd* joined the network's regular schedule of programming on March 10, 2003, airing four nights a week.

Quinn's pal Ken Ober, who hosted the 1980s MTV game show *Remote Control*, which featured Quinn as the sidekick, served as supervising producer of *Tough Crowd*. They filmed the show at Comedy Central's New York studios. A live audience provided much of the Comedy Cellar–inspired, intimate atmosphere that Quinn desired. It also offered a barometer for comedians to see how their jokes went over.

Those who purposely played to the crowd were quickly reproached by Quinn, who disdained ass-kissing and pandering for applause. In a rare practice for a pre-recorded television show, *Tough Crowd* purposely included jokes that bombed. Uncomfortable silences. Boos. Failed humor attempts. These snafus enhanced the show's unvarnished charm.

Instead of pundits or experts, working comedians (who were often friendly with each other off-stage) filled the panel. Their commentary ranged from insightful to uninformed — and often hilarious. *Tough Crowd* captured the confrontational, unpredictable tension of a barroom fight without forgetting the show's comedy club roots.

Marc Maron said that it was 9/11 that "galvanized the tone of *Tough Crowd*." Some Americans blamed all Arabs and argued for total deportation, while others knew this would not solve the problem and disagreed with the racial profiling. But the show allowed for discussion on all sides. Maron explained: "That's what really created the empowerment of that crew of guys that was like, 'We got just as much a right to talk like this as you fucking pussies can sit there and say, "That's not the right way to do things."'"

Greg was one of the four original guest comedians on *Tough Crowd*. It debuted at 11:30 p.m. right after *The Daily Show*. Although billed as a companion piece to Stewart's hit show, *Tough Crowd* was much rougher in both content and format. It served as a working-class foil to the more highbrow *Daily Show*.

"That was the beauty of it," said Nick Di Paolo. "[Colin Quinn] left the warts and all. He did that on purpose. He didn't want it to be slick like *The Daily Show*."

Quinn's strategy hit a chord with many young viewers who didn't always relate to *The Daily Show*. Eli Sairs, a college student who would later become the first Unified Roast Battle Champion, had had almost no exposure to cable television while growing up in Alabama. After enrolling in Ohio University, the 19-year-old devoured hours of Comedy Central programming from his cramped dorm room. *Tough Crowd* spoke to him. For Sairs, *Tough Crowd* was his Grunge Era: a comedy version of the hugely influential and proudly unglamorous musical movement of the 1990s. "It was clearly a free-for-all of ideas," said Sairs, who appreciated that *Tough Crowd* guests could express liberal or conservative viewpoints without getting shouted down for holding an unpopular opinion. "There was no agenda other than to be clever and funny and to talk about social issues freely."

Sairs found Greg's *Tough Crowd* appearances inspiring, and he particularly admired Greg's ability to emphasize funny over smart. "I found comics who were smart and not very funny, or they were funny and kind of stupid," said Sairs, who spent much of his free time studying standup comedy. "And when I came across Greg, he was both smart and funny . . . I was like, 'Oh, here's the blueprint. This is the perfect comedian.'"

Quinn noticed that viewers tuned in to see Greg. "From day one, Greg was the guy that everyone watched," Quinn said. He called Greg the show's preferred panelist, adding, "He was my father's favorite on the show. I wasn't his favorite."

Quinn made Greg a show regular, and he appeared on Tough Crowd once or twice each week. The show was no media darling. A New York Times review that credited Tough Crowd with possessing a more "authentic common touch" than most shows in the comedy/current events genre, nonetheless dismissed it as the "dismal bottom of the heap" of comparable programs. The writer concluded the critical battering by proclaiming: "Tough Crowd looks especially lame because it immediately follows The Daily Show with Jon Stewart, which deserves all the extravagant praise it has gotten." Tough Crowd lacked a snarky, Ivy League vibe, and the show's fervent supporters loved it all the more because of it.

Although Greg had earned degrees from both Columbia and Harvard, he never touted his schooling as a way to make his points appear more valid. Instead, he allowed his opinions—and jokes—to be judged on their own.

Other *Tough Crowd* regulars appreciated Greg's comedic veracity. "He was the best. He was never flustered. He was committed," said Judy Gold. The format suited not only his intelligence and his quick wit but also his tendency to prepare. Elise Czajkowski said: "I think Giraldo saw the possibility of being on TV every night or two times a week. 'I can do this. I can be great at this . . . I can show all my talents in this form.'"

Greg shared a writing office with Di Paolo; Norton and Robinson shared another one. The work ethic varied dramatically between the two pairs of comics. According to Norton, Greg and Di Paolo pumped out copious amounts of material and continuously came up with new ideas for *Tough Crowd*. "Colin would walk in and me and Keith would be asleep," Norton said. "I'd be laid back in my chair with my feet up on the desk. We got very little done." Greg, by contrast, had a compulsion to create new content before each taping.

Nick Di Paolo recalled a specific incident: "It's like an hour before the show. He goes, 'Di Paolo, you're so competitive. Relax.' Then two minutes before show time, I'm going down the stairs to the studio. He's under the staircase jotting down notes just before they're going to introduce us. I go, 'Who the fuck's competitive, Giraldo?' He was laughing."

Greg did his homework and adopted a studious, workmanlike approach to joke writing. Many of the comedians who appeared on *Tough Crowd* appreciated Greg's preparation. Gold credited Greg with inspiring her to "over-prepare" because "he did work so hard and he was so well read." Norton added that "you always knew when you were on the show with him that if you weren't prepared he was just going to run circles around you . . . He would embarrass you." Quinn said: "People would just try to mess with him because he was prepared and he was so good—he was the guy that never let me down . . . He never let the show down."

In an infamous exchange between Greg and Denis Leary on the show, Leary himself remarked about Greg's preparation. The incident occurred on May 7, 2003. Greg and Leary joined Lenny Clarke and Sue Costello on the *Tough Crowd* panel. Quinn steered the conversation to North Korea. Rumors had circulated that the country was developing nuclear weapons and pointing them toward the United States.

The comedians threw around suggestions on how to mitigate Kim Jong-il's destructive tendencies while cracking jokes about his drinking habits and diminutive stature.

"Do you know how short you have to be to have a Napoleon complex in North Korea?" joked Greg about the five-foot-three dictator.

Moments later, Leary more sternly endorsed an American military action against the communist nation. Greg commented that "maybe there's a nonviolent way to solve the whole North Korea thing." Leary interrupted and mocked Greg's point by proclaiming, "There's a nonviolent way to solve a problem with the country that we hate, that hates us, that's got weapons pointed at us? I don't think so."

Without hesitation, Greg replied: "No, you're right, like Russia, for example, that big Russian war."

The audience went silent—processing the sharp comeback—then laughter broke out in the crowd. Meanwhile, Leary looked at Greg stone-faced, pointing his left index finger in Greg's direction.

Moving on with his planned material, Greg proposed that the two nations could temper their grievances by offering economic concessions: "I heard they'll agree to stop building nukes if American women agree to get their nails done at least twice a week."

Leary—displaying no reaction to the manicure joke—accused Greg of over-preparing. "This guy writes so many jokes before the show it's not even funny," said Leary. "Unbelievable. He's got, he's got a pocket full of them."

"That's kind of what we do here, Denis, a little comedy writing," said Greg. This line caused the fatherly Clarke to shout, "I'm not coming back."

Leary countered: "You're the guy in school who did all the homework and then asked if there was any more that needed to be done." To which Greg snapped: "And if you had tried a little comedy writing, maybe your show would still be on the air."

The atmosphere flipped from comedic to combative. With the two alpha males engaged in trash talk, Quinn set one foot on the coffee table that separated Greg and Leary, to play peacemaker. Quinn then said that the segment was over and alluded to a possible scuffle that might take place on the set. Before the lights faded out Quinn said, "This is as ugly as it's gotten, and it definitely gets ugly on this show."

This exchange between Greg and Leary has gone down as an epic moment in the annals of comedy lore. Comedian Steve Hofstetter called it "one of the greatest things I've ever seen." Maron said, "There's no better moment of television that I can imagine."

Once the episode returned from commercial break, no ugliness or tension lingered. The comedians appeared undisturbed and joked almost dispassionately about fraternity hazing.

"Fraternities are great," said Greg, referencing his college days. "If you get drunk and pass out, there's always someone to pee on you."

So why were things so calm? Details behind how the altercation went down add to its mystique. The portion of the show involving North Korea was a *replacement* segment and not part of the original taping. Quinn considered the first version too "boring" and requested a reshoot. The exchange between Greg and Leary was taped last but aired early in the show. So the reordering gave the appearance that nothing had carried over from the fight between Greg and Leary. Greg was concerned about how the substitution of the segments made him look. "He didn't want people to think that he had backed off," said Shillue, who talked with Greg about the dispute after the show. Greg was firm: "I didn't wimp out."

As for Leary, he was more objective about the incident. "It was a great moment, where I really looked like a douchebag," he said in an interview almost eight years after his appearance on *Tough Crowd*. "And I felt bad. In Greg's defense, he actually — he was very prepared for almost anything that could have happened." Quinn granted Leary the opportunity not to air the segment. Leary, however, insisted that it stay in, telling Quinn: "That was good TV."

Opinions vary regarding the long-term effect that the incident had on the rapport between Leary and Greg. Some suggested that they never did reconcile after the confrontation. Shillue said that Greg told him that he "patched it up with Leary right after the show."

Greg also called his friend Steve Klein 15 minutes after the show to share that "something weird happened today" but also that he felt "shocked that what had happened was such a big deal."

Greg's range and style on *Tough Crowd* were wide and varied. He was well-informed and quick-witted. But he never lost sight of his role as a comedian. His focus was on being funny, no matter the topic or circumstance. Norton said:

> *He was always going for the joke. I think the mistake a lot of comedians make is that they think that they have to sound smart, or they think they have to be right, and they forget that being funny is more important than those things. You've got to be original, but you got to be true to being funny before being correct. You can give your opinion, but you should realize that you're going to be wrong half the time. I think the important thing with Greg is that his goal was to be funny and he was a naturally bright guy and he talked about things he wanted to talk about.*

Maron appreciated Greg's contributions to the show: "What he talked about was great because it gave intelligent, brutally honest, crass comedy a platform." Greg never played the role of partisan cheerleader. Czajkowski said: "Giraldo could swing and hit wherever you needed a balance. If you had a lot of far-left people on, he was there to keep really moderate and maybe a little to the right. If you had a lot of right-wing people on, he was there to keep on the left. He could fill in whatever you needed him to be because he was smart enough to argue any side of pretty much any story."

Maron elaborated: "Greg Giraldo was more cut from the cloth of Lenny [Bruce] or [Bill] Hicks in a way in that what you're really looking at is trying to get at a certain truth. Picking sides is not really part of the comedian's job in that. If you're going to be a cultural critic, you should remain relatively sideless and go at both sides pretty evenly."

One of the show's most endearing qualities was how it embraced immature silliness. The comedians proudly lambasted each other. Yes, it was a debate at times, but it wasn't always highbrow or philosophical. Greg enjoyed the schoolyard clowning.

Nick Di Paolo said: "Giraldo could deliver a great joke on religion and then make fun of Patrice's jacket in the same breath. That was the beauty of it. That's what I loved about him. He was a really bright kid, but he never flaunted it or shoved it in your face."

The dynamic between Greg and Patrice O'Neal created some of the most entertaining moments in *Tough Crowd*'s history. The two disagreed on many topics and routinely blasted each other, often insulting one another's appearance and ethnicity.

Nick Di Paolo said that "Giraldo let some doozies go on Patrice that only somebody of Hispanic heritage could get away with. He wasn't afraid to say shit where he could be deemed racist. That's what I liked about him. He wasn't very cautious, and I loved that."

Greg and O'Neal weren't above focusing on the superficial. It made for some incredibly memorable television. Here is a sampling of their exchanges:

> *Patrice*: "Here's why white people are un-cool. They're trying to be black but they still trying to have white style. Like, look at how Colin's dressed—it's corduroy, it's pure trying to be black but trying to keep a whiteness to it. But it fits exactly. Do you see how black people's clothes, they *kind of* fit. Now stand up for a second, Greg, just stand one second. You see how Greg's pants *fit*? That's why I don't like it."

> *Greg*: "By the way, Patrice, it's good to see you've learned to talk without saying 'Hey, hey, hey' first."

> *Patrice*: "That was a good one, independent-film hair. With your planned messiness. Shut up."

> *Greg*: "Well, today is a very sad day. I can't tell whether it's because of the end of the

show, or because of the herd of cattle that died to make Patrice's coat."

Greg: "California, for example, had a test, a written test, which was basically a literacy test—and the NRA is saying that's wrong because there shouldn't be a literacy test to own a gun. If you can't read, you shouldn't own a gun. No offense, Patrice."

Greg: "Of course blacks watch more TV: there's not a hell of a lot to do in jail."

Patrice: "Coming from a Puerto Rican, that really hurts."

The final episode of *Tough Crowd* aired November 4, 2004. During his monologue, Quinn thanked the show's supporters, then praised Richard Pryor's view of comedic integrity, which he defined as "the ability to critique the hypocrisy of society, but to be real enough to see that you are as guilty of it as anyone else in the game."

Quinn then mentioned so-called comedy experts like the *New York Times* critics who slammed the show's guests for their "mean-spirited, sometimes racist, sometimes sexist, sometimes ignorant" comments. "That sounds like every human being I've ever met who's honest with themselves," said Quinn, who supported his friends by adding, "Yes, for these dummies who had the balls to reveal all their ugliness and humanity for the sake of honesty in comedy, let's start the show."

The finale returned a lineup identical to the first episode's (Greg, Di Paolo, Norton, and Robinson), except for the addition of O'Neal. The comedians were as rambunctious and abrasive as they had been for the nearly two years of the series. Robinson said: "We should go out a little better, man, to show our displeasure with them canceling *Tough Crowd*. We should go to *The Daily Show* and whip Jon Stewart's ass. That's what we should do. We should give him his Moment of Zen right upside of his head." Quinn asked a question regarding the media's reluctance to review *Tough Crowd*. With apparent seriousness, Greg responded: "The people that are in the media that review shows are a certain kind of upper-class, elitist type of person. They have a certain view of comedy. This show was more in-your-face, very blue-collar, down-to-earth, honest, not ironically distant, and they didn't know what to make of it."

The conversation later turned to the possibility of Greg's landing a new show on the network. Norton suggested that Quinn and Greg change positions, with Greg hosting and Quinn sitting with the other comedians. They talked Greg into it and he stood up by the pool table to say, "You know what? This is better." It lasted for an uncomfortable but comical 20 seconds until Greg told Quinn to "get back up there." O'Neal, however, showed some genuine emotion. "I just had a moment," said O'Neal who reflected on his time on *Tough Crowd*. "I'm gonna miss everything."

Several *Tough Crowd* regulars have offered reasons for the show's cancellation. Maybe it was a ratings issue. Jim Norton said that the producers not only disagreed ideologically with much of the show's content but also wanted to pigeonhole the comedians into talking only about pop culture — leaving politics to Stewart and race to Dave Chappelle. Norton said that this "was enraging to Colin and to the rest of us because it was like, 'Why is Dave the only one who can talk about race?' I think that they didn't necessarily like where we came from on some of that stuff so they wanted us to stick to pop culture."

Di Paolo didn't mince words when discussing the network heads, describing those who ran Comedy Central at the time as "white cowards who are afraid of their own shadow."

"They really are," said Di Paolo. "How do you think we got to this point where Seinfeld is too edgy?" He related an anecdote about his experience doing standup, where a similar fear prevailed:

> *Last night I was at The Stand, a club in New York, a little tiny club in there, smaller than the friggin' Comedy Cellar. There's two black gentlemen up front probably older than me. They had suit jackets on. They fucking loved me. I*

made a couple cracks about the riots in Baltimore. The rest of the room was fucking Johnny White NYU students. They're getting all nervous and clamming up. The two black guys are howling. I'm talking to them. I said, "Look around," to the black guys. I said, "Look at all the white kids afraid I'm going to hurt your feelings."

In any case, *Tough Crowd* ended. The two years of working on the show were busy and life-changing for Greg. *Tough Crowd* helped him find his comedic voice. It exposed him to a broader national audience and provided a platform for him to showcase his comedic prowess in both writing and performing.

Chapter 7

Pilots, TV Appearances, Movies

On a day-to-day basis, you get tired of waiting to be accepted. In show business, someone else has to say that you're good or that you're worth going to see or worth taping a show.

— Greg Giraldo

Greg enhanced his brand and supplemented his income by making guest appearances on TV and acting in movie projects. He hoped to land a lucrative opportunity, like *Common Law*, that would offer career stability — or at least keep him in the public eye.

Success in show business is unpredictable and Greg often dwelt on the sting of rejection. Colin Quinn said that Greg's intelligence and sensitivity made him more susceptible to show business frustrations. "That used to get to him, just the levels of ignorance in show business," said Quinn. "It gets old. It gets to *anybody* with half a fuckin' brain."

Jim Gaffigan also commented on the amount of rejection in show business and characterized the effect it can have on a performer as a "tax" quite unlike anything experienced by anyone in a regular profession, such as being a lawyer, where objective hard work and long hours will eventually get you the success, the money, and the partnership that you strive for. "In the entertainment industry," Gaffigan said, "the rejection, the television show that didn't work, the second television show that didn't work, the five or six Comedy Central shows that didn't work—there's a tax to that."

There was an extra shock in this for Greg because he had a pattern of success since childhood. He was successful in grade school and college and even in law school. That changed when he was in his late 20s and trying to break into the comedy business. The failures were difficult to stomach. "He was a great comedian," said Gaffigan. "But his track record would have told him that he might *not* be a great comedian."

After the cancellation of *Common Law* in 1996, Greg acted in a couple of movies. He shot several network pilots, appeared on talk shows, and even acted in television commercials. In January of that year, he teamed up with Steve Klein to act in a short film directed by Klein titled *Choices*. The lead characters were modeled after Klein and Greg. This project included nonunion performers, such as a retired ad man who hadn't started acting until his late 60s, whom Klein cast as an old mob boss. The movie wasn't released until 2000.

Greg's second foray into acting was also with Klein as director, but this time in a feature-length film called *Game Day*, starring Richard Lewis. Shooting began in 1997 and finished in 1998. Lewis plays a former Division I college basketball coach who ends up in a small town, coaching a low-quality college team to victory. Klein had Greg in mind when he wrote the part of "Zippy the thug." One interesting detail is that the costume designer for the movie was MaryAnn McAlpin, who would of course become Greg's wife the following year, 1999, when the movie was released.

In 2002, NBC filmed a pilot titled *The Greg Giraldo Show*. Conan O'Brien produced this sitcom, which was based on a standup comedian, played by Greg, who had a son. The set paid homage to the Comedy Cellar — with nods to owner Manny Dworman and booker Estee Adoram, and shots of comedians gathering at a table. Greg's friend Dave Diamond called the pilot episode "very funny" but speculated that the show might have suffered from trying to interweave too many concepts at once. NBC's content restrictions might have weakened the humor as well. "They can't really be that dirty or funny," said Diamond. "Because it's a network show."

Greg had met comedian Nick Swardson in 1997 when they both appeared on *HBO Comedy Showcase* with host Louie Anderson. Greg pushed hard to get Swardson on his pilot and said to him, "Dude, I think you can fucking do this. I'm really pulling for you. Just keep nailing it."

It worked. Swardson got the part. Greg was genuinely excited. Swardson recalled that Greg was not partying hard during this time of his life but instead dedicating himself to making the show a success. "This felt like Greg's moment," said Swardson. "He had Conan O'Brien behind him . . . This was a really hot show. It was a really hot pilot."

The pilot went incredibly well. "It couldn't have gone better," said Swardson, who celebrated with Greg in his L.A. hotel room after the taping finished. Greg enjoyed the occasion by calmly laughing and conversing with guests. Swardson had a less subdued reaction. He celebrated by shouting and throwing lawn furniture off the balcony.

From the outset, insider buzz suggested that *The Greg Giraldo Show* could become NBC's next prime-time hit—joining the ranks of *Friends*, *Will & Grace*, and *Scrubs*. The show's concept meshed well with Greg's off-camera persona. It had the backing of a major network and the endorsement of Conan O'Brien. Greg's acting ability had improved since his experience on *Common Law* six years earlier. Even a skeptic would have given the show a real chance to succeed. But the elation was short-lived. The pilot was not picked up. Instead of Greg's show, NBC chose the pilot for *In-Laws*, produced by Kelsey Grammer, who still had tremendous pull at the network due to the highly successful run of *Frasier*. Greg was devastated.

"Ah, fuck, man," he said to Swardson over the phone. Greg acknowledged that everyone had done their best on the pilot and that the final decision had been out of their hands. "Kelsey had a lot of clout at the network," Greg told Swardson. "Theirs just squeaked ahead of ours."

It had made sense for Greg to feel hopeful, but the high expectations surrounding the project had caused him to lower his usual defenses, making this sting more intense. The rejection hit Greg hard.

"People are in your ear saying, 'Dude, you guys are going to get this. This is your spot. There's no way this isn't going to get picked up' . . . Once you start getting that on repeat in your fucking head . . . that's the second you go, 'Yeah, maybe this is it,' the second you cross that line, the rejection is tenfold," Swardson said.

Greg broke the discouraging news to his wife and children but he moved on from the disappointment. He never landed a major network sitcom again. *Common Law* was the only one to be broadcast nationally.

Nevertheless, television executives wanted Greg in their projects. He had more than half a dozen network deals during his career.

One evening in 2004, Greg performed at a New York City club. He playfully mocked American problems, from marijuana to education. He lampooned the country's priorities and its penchant for overstatement. He addressed the obesity epidemic. "How'd you get through it, Grandpa?" Greg asked the audience while impersonating a curious young boy. "Oh, it was horrible, Johnny," Greg answered.

"There was cheesecake and pork chops everywhere."

In the crowd sat Søren Nystrøm Rasted of the Danish-Norwegian music group Aqua, known for its hit single "Barbie Girl." He and Greg shared a mutual friend. Aqua was planning to launch a side project called Lazyboy, which aimed to produce a spoken-word album. The European pop star was so impressed with Greg's act that he implored him to participate in the new venture. Greg didn't grasp the full extent of Aqua's endeavor. He thought it was a peculiar artistic project involving comedians with a social-commentary bent.

After the show, Greg enjoyed several drinks before meeting up with Rasted at his hotel room, where a portable music studio had been set up. There Greg recorded many of his popular jokes. Upon finishing the session, Greg allegedly received only $800 for his contribution.

In April 2004, Lazyboy released "Underwear Goes Inside the Pants," a spoken-word single that featured nearly five minutes of Greg's material with instrumental accompaniment. No other comedians were included in the song. The single became an international hit—shooting Lazyboy into pop-culture prominence. It reached number five on the Australian singles chart and number 30 in the United Kingdom. American audiences loved it, too. K-Rock played the single every day for more than two weeks — it competed with Green Day releases for the station's most requested song.

Instead of making millions from the song, Greg allegedly didn't receive any money beyond his initial payment in the hotel room. Each time Klein brought up how much Greg should have made, Greg told him that he was making him nauseous and would drive him to drink if he didn't shut up. Comedian Steve Hofstetter hosted a syndicated radio show at the time that broadcast to 172 stations. He wanted to help Greg. Hofstetter emailed Greg, offering to promote "Underwear Goes Inside the Pants." In reply, Greg wrote only, "I made tens of dollars off that song." In a follow-up message, Hofstetter reiterated that he could help Greg benefit from the song and sought Greg's blessing to spread the word to MTV, college radio, and other outlets. But Greg never responded.

"All he ever wanted to do was write standup and perform it," said Hofstetter. His heart was in performing — not advertising or promotion.

About one year after the Lazyboy incident, Greg starred in a series of television commercials for OKCable. These ads featured Greg touting the superiority of cable connectivity over satellite and dial-up options.

In some of the commercials, Greg nondescriptly highlights the benefits of the sponsor. In others he employs his approachable, everyman style of humor. It's uncertain if Greg had a hand in writing the scripts, but his sense of humor shines. Some of his lines include: "You can download videos of your friends and family without waiting. If you don't have friends and family, then it's the best way to listen to really sad music on the internet as you cry yourself to sleep." And: "Don't be a loser and get DSL. DSL sounds like a tendon in your knee."

The OKCable campaign also showcased Greg's bilingualism. He speaks Spanish in some of the 30-second spots and English in others. In one of the Spanish-language commercials, Greg walks through a neighborhood diner discussing the advantages of cable. All the while, Greg speaks in over-the-top, stereotypical voices, mimicking Spanish-language TV stars. Just before the advertisement ends, Greg imitates the accents and slang from various Latin countries saying, "it's good for everyone."

Apart from commercials, Greg also appeared on TV talk shows — as a guest, host, or performer. During the last decade of his career, Greg appeared on several high-profile shows including *Late Night with Conan O'Brien* and the *Late Show with David Letterman*. For a couple of years, Greg had a recurring gig on *Last Call with Carson Daly*, providing "merciless pop-culture commentary, skewering such worthy targets as 'Gigli' ('I haven't even seen it yet, and I already want my 10 bucks back') and Melissa Joan Hart's wedding-themed reality show ('I'd watch that if my other choice was drinking pig urine')." But Greg made guest appearances on a wide range of other shows including *The View*, *The Howard Stern Show*, *The Wanda Sykes Show*, and Dave Attell's *Gong Show*.

Greg knew the value of appearing on such shows. For a comedian, perhaps the apex of promotional payoff was the *Letterman* show. Greg tried to get on it many times. In an interview with Howard Stern in 2004, he mentioned that he did manage to score the booking—but the great Letterman was away and Regis Philbin guest-hosted. That was February 28, 2003, and Greg joked about the event: "I got on the show once when Regis Philbin was hosting. That's really a dream come true."

He also experienced some of the difficult realities of television, especially in his attempts to get on the *Letterman* show while Letterman was actually hosting. Greg was bumped several times in 2004 and 2005. He was scheduled to appear, showed up at the studio, but did not perform because some other segment went long. He was bumped for Rosie Perez, and then General Tommy Franks, and the third time for Jane Pauley. Greg did not take this well. He got paid for showing up, but he had to forgo money he would have made from performing on the road and, more importantly, he missed the chance to showcase his comedy to tens of millions of viewers.

The long-time booker on *Letterman*, Eddie Brill, tried to reassure Greg that getting bumped was nothing personal. Brill told Greg that Letterman had no animus toward him. Letterman just didn't keep track of the time each guest occupied. If a segment with another guest seemed to be going well, *Late Show* producers would let it continue — and eat up Greg's scheduled time.

"Greg, it has nothing to do with you, you're a great comic," Brill told him when Perez was the guest on July 31, 2004, but the rejection hit Greg's insecurities. He was hurt. He was angry.

During the third time, with Pauley, on September 3, 2004, Greg was particularly upset, and so was Letterman. A production assistant pushed Greg out on stage while the show was on a commercial break. This surprised Letterman, who knew there was no time left for Greg to appear. In any case, Greg walked to the desk and Letterman asked him about his upcoming weekend performances. Greg — too angry to provide details — answered curtly, "You know what, I don't even know" — to which Letterman replied, "Well, way to sell tickets."

Greg finally made it on the show with Letterman there and got to perform standup about six months later, on March 4, 2005. Some resentment from the prior three bumps still lingered for Greg, but he had an inspired set. The studio audience loved his performance. Letterman came over to shake hands with Greg, which was his customary gesture to thank comedians. Greg didn't outright rebuff the handshake. But he turned away from Letterman. It may have been an intentional slight or possibly an unconscious act, or it may even have been a deferential move on Greg's part—but it was something that Letterman and the producers noticed.

The sting from the Letterman incident may have stuck with Greg for a while. The next evening, he headlined the Zipper Factory's Monday night "Eating It" show. Greg lacked his usual vigor and energy on stage. Journalist Conor Hogan, who attended the show, found Greg's performance below his usually high standard. "He was just a little off," said Hogan. "He was just out of gas that night . . . He just seemed kind of exhausted and not excited to be there." Hogan attributed the lackluster performance to Greg's appearance on *Letterman*: "He was just tired and mentally exhausted from what I'm sure was an anxiety-filled performance on the Letterman show."

About a month later, on April 7, 2005, Greg shot a pilot for a second show called *The Greg Giraldo Show*, this time for Comedy Central. It was similar to *Tough Crowd*, and designed to follow *The Daily Show*. *Daily Variety* reported:

> *Untitled project, shot last month in New York, featured Giraldo and three other panelists weighing in on news, sports, politics and other headlines of the day. First two segments are dedicated to discussion of different issues, while the last third is a man-on-the-street-style field segment from Giraldo. In the pilot, for example, Giraldo chatted up gymgoers about steroids.*

Greg felt guilty about the *Tough Crowd* cancellation. He also worried that if Comedy Central gave him the show, it might look like a slight to Colin Quinn. But Quinn urged Greg to take advantage of the opportunity, telling him: "You've got to do it. It's not like you're taking my show. I've already been in that position. You do what's in front of you. You're not sabotaging. You didn't go behind my back."

Patrick Milligan, founder of CringeHumor.com and later the vice-president at CH Entertainment, sat in on the taping of the pilot. This version of *The Greg Giraldo Show* was shot in the same studio and on the same set as *Tough Crowd*. Managers and staff from Quinn's show also worked on this one, compounding the already obvious similarities between the two programs. "It was creepy," Milligan wrote. "It was Greg Giraldo and a panel of four," but it didn't have the same feel at all as *Tough Crowd*. "Greg was brilliant; he was sharp as a tack. But everyone was respectful of each other. No one talked over each other, no one stepped on anyone's lines. The camera would go to them and they would talk and that was it. And it didn't capture that essence that *Tough Crowd* had," wrote Elise Czajkowski.

This is what Milligan wrote about Greg's performance: "Dressed in all black, with his patented 'messy yet neat' hairstyle, Greg grabs the mic and points out familiar faces from the past scattered all throughout the audience . . . He blurts out the words 'Tough Crowd' and is met with a genuine round of applause . . . He looks over in my direction and blurts out something to the effect of 'I don't want to read on Cringe Humor that this is just a second-rate *Tough Crowd.*'"

The show proceeded, and the panel of comedians included Lewis Black, Lynne Koplitz, and Patton Oswalt. As Milligan described it, "the big guns for tonight—two Comedy Central legends, and a gorgeous comedienne to help break up what would otherwise be a sausage fest." The various issues debated included "homosexual overtones in children's entertainment" and the use of steroids in baseball. The show mimicked the format of *Tough Crowd*, but to Milligan, it didn't "capture the same vibe":

> *Even though there are similar elements, I don't see it happening. The show has an odd West Coast vibe about it. Everything is just too rehearsed & pristine. It probably came off that way, because after all, it was a pilot that's being sold to the network. Everything had to be perfect as people's jobs are on the line. The beauty of Colin's show was the unpredictable element presented when you had 2–3 buddies in comedy interacting with timid outsiders. Seeing the old regulars harass the outsiders & one another is what myself and the majority of the CH fan base loved seeing. You never saw that realism on a show before. It can never be captured again.*

In the end, the show was another pilot that didn't materialize. Once again, Greg missed a big break. He had grown accustomed to tempering his family's expectations about such missed opportunities. Nevertheless, Greg loathed seeing disappointment in the people he was trying so desperately not to disappoint.

More pilots came down the pipeline for Greg. One from Comedy Central called *Gone Hollywood* never aired. In fact, it was converted into another show and hosted by a different comedian. Jon Lafayette reported that the show had been "sent back to the shop for a few tweaks," including the replacement of Greg as host. Ultimately, David Spade became the new host for a series that Comedy Central re-christened *The Showbiz Show with David Spade*. It launched in September 2005. This program, which lasted 13 episodes, borrowed heavily from Spade's snarky persona made popular by his "Hollywood Minute" segments on *Saturday Night Live*'s "Weekend Update."

Comedy Central found another project for Greg to host: *Stand-Up Nation*, which was originally called *Friday Night Stand-Up* when it debuted in 2005. The network apparently gave him this opportunity because it "didn't want to fuck over Greg." It lasted until 2007, about as long as the *Showbiz Show*, and it was a financial success for Greg because it was based on the deal for *Gone Hollywood*.

Another pilot, in 2007, was called *Adult Content* (it's available as an extra on the *Midlife Vices* DVD). It starts with a close-up on Greg, who says: "So here's the idea: it's a comedy show about sex. It'll be great. It's a topic everyone can relate to. And it won't be gratuitous or lowbrow humor. I'm not talking about a bunch of cheap sex jokes. I'm talking about a smart look at the state of sexuality in contemporary American society." A screen goes down, Greg says "Ah shit," and then it's revealed that he's at a peep show talking to a stripper. The screen goes up, he asks her, "So what do you think?" and she replies with a very bored "Whatever."

The rest of the 20-minute episode consists of an opening warm-up standup bit, and segments on the spiritual side of sexuality (including an interview with a woman who provides "sex toys for Christian married couples"), sex-toys prohibition, Craigslist personal ads, a "Three-Way" interview with two female sex experts on oversexualized culture, and, finally, "sexual positions from the Kama Sutra demonstrated by giant pandas" (during the credits).

The following year Greg starred in the U.S. pilot for *Caiga Quien Caiga*, a weekly comedy show that became a hit on Argentine television. Panelists commented on current events and interviewed public figures. The one-hour pilot featured segments with presidential candidates Barack Obama and John McCain as well as an interview with Danny

Bonaduce and a red-carpet segment at the MTV Movie Awards.

And there was supposed to be one additional pilot show around this time that unfortunately didn't even get shot. It might have been the most appropriate for Greg's talents. The premise was that Greg hosted a tell-it-like-it-is radio talk show. "That pilot really captured his voice well," said Steve Klein.

In addition to the pilots, Greg also signed several retainer contracts with networks throughout his career. These are generally referred to as "holding deals," in which Greg received a fee for a show that a network might develop. Dina Appleton and Daniel Yankelevits wrote in *Hollywood Dealmaking*: "The purpose of the commitment is to (1) hold the actor off the market for a limited period of time in an attempt to cast the actor in one of the many pilots being developed for the network, or (2) in the case of higher-level performers, to keep them off the market in order to develop a project specifically for them."

Greg had holding deals almost every year, a rare circumstance for standup comedians. "Not everybody gets a holding deal year every year," said Dave Diamond. "Not everybody gets to shoot three pilots." In spite of his success in landing these deals, Greg was fairly ambivalent about whether he wanted many of the projects to materialize. He also had apprehensions about moving to Los Angeles. "I don't think he was ever one hundred percent sure that he really wanted to get a show," said Diamond. "He would have liked the money, but I think he always thought that comedy was so much better in New York . . . and he thought California was very artificial."

Chapter 8
The Roasts

Jeff Ross, I remember the exact moment you became the best roaster in the room. It was when Greg Giraldo died.
— Natasha Leggero

The concept of a roast is simple. Each roaster has the opportunity to lampoon the guest of honor, the other roasters, the emcee, and anyone else on the dais. The honored guest takes the stage last and returns the same insult-laden treatment back to the performers. Roasts celebrate raunchy, off-color humor. Comedians compete to push the limits of propriety. Roasts are not to everyone's taste. Audience members may take offense at certain jokes. Participants can interpret playful digs as genuine criticism. Networks can lose advertisers. Comedy critics may declare that a line was crossed.

The New York Friars Club began roasting honorees in the 1950s. The Friars held dear the notion that you only roast the ones you love. Most of the roasters were close to the "victim." That changed decades later on the Comedy Central roasts. Comedians and celebrities who didn't know the guest personally were allowed to participate. The Comedy Central roastees have varied from Flavor Flav to Donald Trump to Justin Bieber. The roasters range from experienced comedians, such as Jeff Ross, Greg Giraldo, and Lisa Lampanelli, to other celebrities, including Snoop Dogg, Peyton Manning, and even *Jersey Shore*'s The Situation.

From 1998 to 2002, Comedy Central aired five Friars Club roasts. After five years, the agreement between the Friars Club and Comedy Central ended. In 2003 Comedy Central inked a deal with Denis Leary's production company, Apostle. Frank DiGiacomo reported: "Though the partnership had been extremely lucrative to the Friars, they seemed relieved to be free of the yoke of national television. No longer did they have to lard the dais with young observational comics for the sake of demographics, or deal with big-name comedy stars who were afraid of working blue on national cable television."

The first of the revamped Comedy Central roasts aired in 2003. Robert Kelly traced the origin of these shows to a roast of club owner Barry Katz that took place at the Boston Comedy Club in New York: "Jeff Ross sold the idea to Comedy Central. It was just us celebrating each other and smashing each other. It was pretty fucking great. It was at a little club, just us, mostly comics. Some industry, a little fans. To me, it's what roasts are all about."

Greg performed in nine of the roasts that aired on Comedy Central: Chevy Chase in 2002, Jeff Foxworthy and Pamela Anderson in 2005, William Shatner in 2006, Flavor Flav in 2007, Bob Saget in 2008, Larry the Cable Guy and Joan Rivers in 2009, and David Hasselhoff in 2010.

Comedians and comedy fans revere Greg as one of the best roasters ever. His intelligence, writing skills, ability to ad-lib, and his lack of concern at being offensive all came together. The results were hilarious.

Many knew Greg as "the guy from the roasts." The shows enhanced his notoriety, but they may have detracted from his broader standup talents. To fervent fans, calling Greg a roast comedian is like calling Michael Jordan a slam-dunk champion. Roasts were an exhibition where Greg excelled, but they did not encompass his overall comedic style.

"He was *not* an insult comic," remarked Noam Dworman, manager of the Comedy Cellar in New York's Greenwich Village: "So he got this opportunity to do these roasts and, of course, he was the best at it. That was a big platform; all of a sudden 20 times more people saw him than had ever seen him before. Now he becomes an insult comic in people's minds. That was the least of his things and not at all what anybody who really knew him admired about him."

Dworman added: "[Greg] really was an heir to George Carlin. He could talk about heavy issues without being preachy and dissect them and have his own insight and make them funny."

Ted Alexandro, who performed regularly at the Comedy Cellar, agreed. Alexandro argued that Greg's talents were underused in the format—that the roasts were "beneath him." He felt disappointed that Greg's talents were used by a system to make fun of dented celebrities.

"It's not a judgment of him or Flavor Flav or the culture," said Alexandro. "I guess that's the most easily disposable type of entertainment. Pick a person like Charlie Sheen, who has a meltdown, put him in a roast."

Greg, nonetheless, enjoyed the roasts. The fast-paced, current-events focus played well to his comedic sensibilities. He combined edgy and clever material and loved to push boundaries. He appreciated the challenges the roasts presented. However, he never made insult comedy a staple of his road act.

In traditional standup comedy, performers work out material at live venues. Roasts do not afford the same type of preparation opportunities. This makes it difficult for performers to gauge how their jokes will be received.

Greg would run joke ideas by trusted sources including Jesse Joyce, a comedian 13 years younger than him who frequently opened for Greg on the road.

Joyce shared: "Roast writing is such a specific, niche skill in comedy. There are guys . . . who are hilarious who are just not roast joke writers. It's a real specific animal . . . It's one of the things you don't know if you're good at it until you actually try it."

Steve Klein, one of Greg's allies for testing his material, said, "He would call me and read down a list of jokes and get my *yay* or *nay* on them. It would be a week outside the roast and he's like, 'I fucking haven't written a thing yet.' He would come up with all that shit literally a couple of days before or the day of." As Greg's roast experience grew, he relied more on his comedic instincts and less on the input of his friends. He still worked feverishly on each show, taking the opportunity seriously.

Greg debuted his insult-comedy stylings to a national TV audience at the Chevy Chase roast in 2002. Most of the performers, including Greg, didn't know Chase personally. This show lacked the friendly camaraderie common to most roasts. It took more than seven hours to tape the show. This long production time created angst among the cast and crew.

Chase was so pissed off that he didn't bother to meet with any of the performers before the show. This move helped build an uncomfortable tension that lingered throughout the roast.

Paul Shaffer, the host, looked around the dais and said, "These are all unknowns. This is gonna suck. These are nobodies."

Greg played off that line during his set saying, "Yes, I'm a nobody, but at least I'm a nobody at the beginning of my career" — a clear dig at Chase's fallen star power.

During his performance, Greg continued to assault Chase, commenting that Chase's talk show aired for six weeks while Sally Jesse Raphael's lasted 16 years. Raphael, sitting on the dais, yelled out, "Twenty." Demonstrating his sharp off-the-cuff ability, Greg replied, "Oh, fuck you, I chopped off four years for symmetry. Shut up. Twenty? It felt like 40."

Chevy Chase didn't enjoy the roast. After production wrapped, he went on a long rant about what a horrible experience it had been. Greg later shared: "Chevy Chase was one of the first roasts I did and the whole time he was there he was angry. When they did roasts back in the '70s they were attended by all these A-list celebrities and our roast wasn't. He was just angry at the whole thing and we were there telling all these jokes to a guy who just wasn't into it."

In spite of Chase's bitterness, Greg's propensity for the put-down was on display. And comedians were floored by his breakout performance. Andy Kindler, who participated in the roast, marveled at Greg's ability to weave honesty and hilarity with the right kind of meanness. "Nobody could have foreseen how amazing he was, like it was his natural skin to insult people," Kindler said.

Greg joined his New York buddies to perform on smaller-scale roasts. In 2003, Rich Vos hosted a roast of Patrice O'Neal at the Boston Comedy Club in Greenwich Village. Unlike the Chevy Chase roast, this event had a friendly combativeness to it, like a close family arguing at dinner. During Greg's introduction, Vos mentioned that Greg had participated in several sitcoms but "his last one, though, was canceled during the table read."

About a minute into his act, Greg addressed Vos's recent appearance on *Last Comic Standing*. Greg said, "If you stay positive and work hard for 20 years, you can beat out six open mic-ers for a spot on the most degrading show in the history of television."

Greg continued to dig into his friends. On Robert Kelly, who used video equipment during his set: "He's used to carrying a lot of shit. All Dane Cook's golf clubs." Then to Jim Norton: "How do you insult a guy who hires hookers to piss in his face? What do you say? His chin has seen more noxious fluids than Lisa Lampanelli's panty shields." Greg went easy on Colin Quinn. After praising Quinn's humor and insightfulness, Greg lobbed a softball at his *Tough Crowd* boss. Referencing the hate mail Quinn received during the show, Greg said, "And I didn't agree with any of it except for the stuff about him being gay." This caused O'Neal to berate Greg from the crowd. "What kind of fucking ass-kissing shit was that, motherfucker?" said O'Neal. "Say something mean, bitch . . . You told him he was wonderful, you fucking cocksucker. It's a roast. Roast him!"

Some back-and-forth ensued with O'Neal before Greg mentioned Colin Quinn's engagement: "Colin

Quinn is getting married. Those are five words I never expected to hear — like 'Comedy Central presents Keith Robinson.'"

The closing minutes were dedicated to O'Neal, whom Greg dubbed the "manatee of the hour." Greg described being approached by hordes of *Tough Crowd* fans who asked the same thing about Patrice: "Who's that big fat cunt sitting next to you ... that uninformed, worthless bag of shit?" Greg insisted that he always defended O'Neal. He told them, "You gotta remember, the camera adds 10 pounds."

The momentum Greg built continued in 2005 with the roast of Pamela Anderson. Earlier that year, producer Joel Gallen had connected with Dan Mathews, a vice-president at PETA, and Anderson for lunch in Santa Monica. The trio discussed ideas to raise money for PETA on its 25th anniversary. "We want to roast Pam," Mathews said. "She's agreed to do it, and we want to do it as a fundraiser for PETA."

Gallen responded, "Wow, that's good. We could do it that way, or we can walk into Comedy Central."

Instead of a traditional fundraiser at a private party, Gallen wanted Comedy Central to produce a televised roast. The show's proceeds would go to PETA. Mathews and Anderson loved the idea. Gallen knew Doug Herzog, the president of Viacom (which owned Comedy Central) very well and felt confident Comedy Central would accept his pitch. He was right. He walked into Herzog's office and Comedy Central effectively bought the show in the room.

Gallen scoured videos to find people to appear on the Pam Anderson roast. He watched previous Comedy Central roasts. Greg stuck out. Gallen said, "We've got to have this guy. I started really studying who were the best comics for the roast, and Greg was obviously number one."

Gallen picked up his phone and offered a spot to Greg. He accepted. This agreement paved the way for more of Greg's epic roast performances. It also marked the beginning of a close friendship between Gallen and Greg.

The Pamela Anderson roast, filmed at the Sony Studios in Los Angeles, had the atmosphere of a Las Vegas bachelor party. Women. Booze. Dick jokes. Tommy Lee, Anderson's ex, attended. Roastmaster Jimmy Kimmel, Jeff Ross, and others riffed on the leaked Tommy and Pam sex tape. Hugh Hefner, flanked by Playboy Bunnies, added to the sex-drugs-and-rock-'n'-roll mystique. Andy Dick also celebrated the ribald humor.

Gallen wanted Greg to perform first. "[Greg] packed so much into his material that he was such an entertaining guy to watch," Gallen said. "He had the benefit of going first because all the material was fresh and nothing was really used up." The producers had their home run hitter bat leadoff.

"Our first roaster tonight is part of our very successful Invite a Random Person to the Roast Program," announced Kimmel. "Please welcome the virtually anonymous Greg Giraldo."

"That was great, Jimmy," Greg replied. "I've never seen you be funny on TV before." After a barrage of shots at Adam Carolla, Eddie Griffin, Courtney Love, and Sarah Silverman, Greg addressed Pamela Anderson: "I love you, Pam . . . Watching you in that sex tape was like a whole new experience for me, because up until then I'd never seen anyone *get* gonorrhea before."

Greg touched on Anderson's growing celebrity and jam-packed schedule: "You're busier than Courtney Love's pharmacist." Commenting on Anderson's TV show, *Stacked*, Greg joked, "You starring in a show about books and reading is like Tom Cruise starring in a show about vaginas."

Anderson, the consummate good sport, rolled with the smears. She enjoyed Greg's performance. After his set, Greg and Anderson shared a warm embrace.

Courtney Love added an unforgettable component to the roast. The comics could not help but make fun of her. Love didn't take the ribbing in silence. She blasted back. Between cigarette puffs, Love heckled the comedians, flipped off the crowd, flashed her underwear, pulled up her top, and created a wonderfully memorable spectacle.

During her set, Sarah Silverman quipped, "I was curious to see which Courtney Love was going to show up: the smeared-lipstick crazy coke whore or the violent smeared-lipstick crazy coke whore."

Love almost missed the show. It took Gallen's cajoling to convince her to attend. "I had to spend two nights before the roast after rehearsal going to the Sunset Marquis bar and trying to talk Courtney Love into doing the show," Gallen said. "Which I'm thankful I was able to do because she was such a key element to that show."

Howard Stern would occasionally feature roasts on his radio show. In 2006 *The Howard Stern Show* planned the roast of Gary Dell'Abate, commonly known as Baba Booey, Stern's longtime producer and popular sidekick. They wanted Greg to participate. Erik Lievano, the cousin of Greg's wife and a fervent Howard Stern fan, asked to meet up with Greg in New York for the Baba Booey roast. Greg obliged. Lievano connected with Greg in the lobby of the 51-floor skyscraper on Sixth Avenue in Manhattan that housed the *Howard Stern* studios. Greg escorted Lievano through security, and the two went up to the green room at the show. There they connected with other roasters, including Lisa Lampanelli, Jackie "The Joke Man" Martling, Artie Lange, Greg Fitzsimmons, and Colin Quinn.

"I basically kept my mouth shut and sat back like a fly on the wall—just watched and listened," said Lievano. "It was surreal."

Once the roast began, Lievano stood right behind producer Fred Norris for a front-row seat. Compared to televised roasts, this event had a more raw and edgy feel to it.

Comedian Bob Levy emceed. He brought up Greg with a dig about using his lawyer background to sue the bastard that had thought he was funny enough to make it as a comedian. Greg took the jab in stride and calmly opened his act by taking shots at some of the roasters. He looked at Quinn and said, "Colin, I love you. But you're so washed up, parents now tell their kids to 'Colin Quinn' before supper."

Howard Stern and the rest of the crowd gasped and applauded as Greg plowed into Quinn and others, including Jackie Martling, a veteran comic best known for his work on the Stern show.

"I loved your book, Jackie. *How to Fuck Up a Career You Didn't Deserve in the First Place,*" Greg said.

Martling retorted, "Thank you, Geraldo," referencing the talk show host Geraldo Rivera. Greg quickly followed with, "You're welcome, Oprah."

Turning his attention to another old friend, Greg said, "Greg Fitzsimmons is here to make me feel famous." Greg then ridiculed Lisa Lampanelli and Robin Quivers before targeting Artie Lange. After referencing Lange's drug use, Greg broke out the sharp daggers for Lange's heroin exploits: "You sure as fuck couldn't find a vein in that walrus carcass of yours," Greg said. "You must have just dumped it on your bed and rolled around in it."

Greg saved his most scathing takedown for Baba Booey himself. Earlier that year, Dell'Abate's father had passed away. Stern had missed the wake to take his girlfriend, Beth Ostrosky, to the hospital to tend to her injured foot.

"Gary, I wouldn't have missed this for the world. And the only way Howard would have missed it is if your dead father was lying here."

Dell'Abate, Stern, and the rest in attendance gasped, groaned, and then laughed for about 15 seconds — reeling in the fact that Greg had hit on one of the most publicized show controversies in recent months.

After Greg wrapped up his set, Baba Booey said, "That was a well-crafted, clever, dead-father joke. I totally approve of those. It's great. That's the funniest joke today."

Fitzsimmons, who also had an incredibly well-received set, explained: "You're trying not to bomb, basically. In roasts, the audience is looking at you like you're either going to kill or you're going to bomb and there's nothing in between. Howard Stern is sitting literally 15 feet in front of you staring right at you. It's pretty nerve wracking. You're very much aware of you have to take every single person down on the roast. Not just the roastee but everybody else that's on the dais."

When Comedy Central began producing its own roasts, many of the celebrity performers had no joke-writing experience. So the network hired writers to help the non-standups. This team composed enough jokes to assist all the performers. Non-comedians got first dibs on this material. As the deadline neared, the standup comics could go through the remaining jokes to enhance their acts. The comedians usually ended up with the edgier jokes, ones the celebrities didn't have the desire or the courage to use.

Greg enjoyed pushing the limits of acceptability. He defended himself against those who took his jokes too seriously. During the Bob Saget roast, in 2008, Greg said about Norm Macdonald: "Norm's got a giant gambling problem. He's dropped more coin in a casino than Michael J. Fox at a parking meter." There was a gasp from the audience, to which Greg replied, not missing a beat: "It's a fucking *roast*, groany-groan-groan." His joke about Jerry Springer at the Hasselhoff roast, referring to a video of a drunken Hasselhoff eating a cheeseburger while sitting on the floor, also caused an audible stir in the crowd. Greg said: "You were an aide to Bobby Kennedy, which probably explains your connection to Hasselhoff. I guess you like to hang around guys whose careers end on a hotel floor." The crowd groaned, but Greg just shook his head and said: "That's a good fucking joke, everybody. It's what we call roasting. Anyway, I'm sorry if the meanness has piled up, but that's what we do here."

Katt Williams, who emceed the Flavor Flav roast, took issue with some of the show's content. Greg had skewered him pretty well: "Katt, you're like Afro Sheen: some white people have heard of you, but no one knows what you do." At that first joke, Williams appeared uncomfortable, nodding his head, looking downward, adjusting his clothing. And after Greg finished with, "What a teeny little pimp. Man, being a pimp ain't easy, especially when you got to stand on phonebooks to smack a bitch," Williams was still nodding, noticeably unsmiling, and pretending to act unaffected by it all while casually scratching his ear.

Williams "disowned that roast after the fact," said Joyce. "He has on a bunch of occasions on stage bitched about how he got tricked into doing the roast and he had no idea it was going to be that racist and whatever. And the only thing is, he seemed fine with it at the time, but I think maybe he got flak for it and then as a result had to really distance himself from it."

The celebrities being roasted usually provided a list of forbidden topics. Saget, for example, requested that no one joke about his former *Full House* co-stars the Olsen twins. Joan Rivers had one stipulation—do not make fun of her daughter, Melissa. But one of Greg's jokes involved Melissa Rivers. While it did not make the televised version, the bit sparked controversy on the set—halting production for several minutes. In the joke, Greg compared common traits between Joan Rivers and Michael Jackson. Greg said that they had the same plastic surgeon, they each spent millions to look like a creepy old white lady, and they both raised a chimp. Upon hearing the last line, Melissa Rivers, who was not on the dais, stormed off the set. She eventually returned after the show's producers agreed to cut that joke from the televised show and let Melissa Rivers share a few words.

Jesse Joyce, who wrote the joke, related the story: "When you watch the roast all she does is go up to the mic and go like, 'Hey, thank you, guys, here for coming to honor my mom, and fuck you, Greg Giraldo.' That's all she said, and the only reason that it's there is because of the joke that I wrote. I was really proud of that."

Greg excelled at the roasts, so much so that for all except his first and last appearances he received the coveted distinction of being the first roaster. Going first annoyed Greg. He viewed it as a slap in the face. But others knew the value of going first. It highlighted the best performer and gave him a chance to do jokes and cover topics before anyone else. Greg benefited from an attentive audience. Production could take several hours, and audiences tired as the show went on.

Nick Di Paolo suggested to Greg that he should try to go on early. "Like an idiot, I tell him that," said Di Paolo. "Every other roast after that, he went first. It was in his contract. I'm like, 'Motherfucker. I'm putting it in my contract.'"

The secret to Greg's success at the roasts was not just about going up first. As he had done throughout his career, Greg concentrated on writing. He treated the roasts seriously. "He kept cool and nobody did their homework better on those roasts than he did. He really, really worked hard," said Greg Fitzsimmons. For the Comedy Central roasts, Greg worked with Joyce to co-write some of his material, and it resulted in a very successful partnership, producing some of the roasts' funniest moments.

The first roast that Greg and Joyce worked on together was the roast of Flavor Flav in 2007. Greg knew he had the roast coming up and asked Joyce to write some jokes for him. Greg told Joyce, "If you think of anything, toss it my way." Joyce took the invitation to heart and wrote a copious amount of material. "I just submitted to him like a dozen pages of jokes," said Joyce, who had no idea how Greg would react. "He was like, 'Holy shit. I didn't know you were going to do all this.' He read through them and was like, 'Dude, a lot of these are really great.' That was really validating," said Joyce.

The next year, Greg and Joyce worked together on the Saget roast. The two pitched ideas to one another, from rough premises to specific jokes. They discussed what worked and brainstormed how to fine-tune their ideas. The two crafted one of the roast's most memorable jokes, which involved Saget's appearance. While driving in a car, Joyce pointed out that Saget looked like the Vlasic pickle stork. From the passenger seat, Greg added, "Yeah, you're like the Vlasic pickle stork, except instead of delivering babies, you're not funny."

After Greg gave that tag, Joyce could only muster an astonished "Ah, dude" in reply before laughing loudly.

In 2009 Joyce and Greg teamed up on the Larry the Cable Guy roast. This time, Joyce took a more active role in drafting Greg's set. During the first few minutes of his set, Greg kept true to form. He used clever lines and intelligent prose to bash the redneck comic. Standing behind the podium, Greg said, "Larry fucked his first cousin when he was 16, and his last one about an hour ago."

However, an unscripted outburst by Greg may have been the most unforgettable part of the show.

In a moment of exasperation, Greg yelled: "How the fuck are you so *popular*? Jesus fucking Christ, this one finally broke my back." The audience laughed and applauded Greg's honesty.

"It was just a genuine emotion, really in the moment," said Joyce. "I think that's why it stuck with everybody."

Greg finished his Larry the Cable Guy set with more scripted material.

"You make more money in a week than I'll make in my life," said Greg. "You say you've never done drugs but watching your success has put me in rehab twice. So thanks for ripping my soul out, you hillbilly fuck."

Both Joyce and Greg were recovering alcoholics, and they first became sober within two weeks of each other in 2005. Joyce followed the Alcoholics Anonymous program and managed to avoid alcohol. By the time he and Greg were working on their last roast together, Greg was drinking again.

Greg's situation was serious—so much so that Joyce had to contrive a story about a phony deadline for the Hasselhoff roast in 2010 to get Greg on a plane to Los Angeles. Although Joyce wrote several jokes in advance of the roast, some in Greg's camp grew concerned that Greg was not in the right state of mind to perform. Greg's agent alerted Joyce that Greg might need help. "You gotta get over to his place. He's not himself," the agent told Joyce, who hadn't heard from Greg in a couple of days.

When Joyce arrived at Greg's apartment, he noticed that Greg had broken lamps and punched a hole in the wall. His agent had bought two plane tickets and suggested they try to convince Greg that the roast was the next day (instead of nearly a week away). They went with it. Joyce hid Greg's phone and altered the calendar in Greg's apartment to better sell the ruse. Then he checked Greg's pockets to make sure he didn't have any illegal substances in them. They didn't pack any luggage.

"We'll just get clothes when we get there," Joyce said to Greg, who agreed without protest.

Greg and Joyce went straight to the airport. Once they landed in Los Angeles, a chauffeur drove them to their hotel.

The next morning at breakfast Joyce told Greg the truth. "We have good news," Joyce said. "We have five days to get this together."

At first, Greg was irritated by what had happened. Then he realized what an excellent move it was for his career. He and Joyce spent those five days holed up in the hotel applying the finishing touches to their jokes for the roast—the last they would work on together.

When showtime arrived, Greg was ready. He still didn't want to perform first. Several of the staff writers grumbled that he would burn up all the best jokes at the outset. So he approached the producers about getting a different spot in the lineup. They listened. He closed the show.

Seth MacFarlane introduced Greg, and he crushed. He riffed on Pamela Anderson and tore into Hasselhoff's rumored drinking problem. "When alcohol does its taxes, it claims you as a dependent," Greg snidely remarked. "Your liver is so shriveled, black, and dead, if you put your ear to your side, you can hear it go, 'Watchu talkin 'bout, Willis?'"

146

Greg as Practical Joker

We were in Dallas and he was going to give me money for working on a roast. He owed me a couple hundred bucks. Somebody had sent him, as a joke, a rubber fuckable ass. It had suction cups, and you would put it on the edge of a table. It was really silly. He just had it sitting on the table, so I was making fun of him about it. Then the next day we went to lunch and he was like, "Dude, you know what's crazy? I used that and it's fucking amazing." He started talking about how great the fuckable ass thing was and how it was going to save his marriage.

So then later that night he was like, "Oh, by the way, I owe you five hundred bucks. So swing by my room and come get it." So I come over and we're talking for two minutes. He goes, "Oh yeah, I got your money. It's on the table." He had shoved it into the fuckin' asshole of the rubber thing, which is like he'd been fucking this table all week long. So I had to get a pen and fuckin' scoop fuckin' hundred-dollar bills out of the ass of a fuckin' rubber sex toy . . . I don't know. I just thought it was really funny. Those are the things that I remember about him that really crack me up.

— *Jesse Joyce*

Greg's roast performances impressed comedian Nick Swardson. "It was just great to watch somebody that had no filter and no barriers," said Swardson. "The longer he did it, the more he really didn't give a fuck."

Swardson added: "It was like a wrecking ball. Greg came in and nobody else who was on the dais compared to Greg. I mean, everybody else would do great, but Greg came in and it was like everybody was just waiting to hear Greg's thoughts because it was so honest and it was so funny."

Swardson knew Greg's talents and avoided the public flogging that might stem from a Greg Giraldo roast. "They would offer me the roast at the beginning all the time, they'd be like, 'You want to be in the roast?'" said Swardson. "I was like, 'No,' and Greg was one of the reasons . . . I've got so many things in my closet, literally, that I don't want Greg's take on my life."

Other networks joined in the roast game. TBS aired the roast of Cheech & Chong in 2008. It lacked the fanfare of other roasts, but Greg still stole the show. Gene Pompa, who attended the event, said: "Everybody ate it except for Greg. Greg basically saved the fucking roast. No one was doing jack, but Greg was such a pro at that." One of Greg's more memorable jokes of the night targeted Cheech Marin, a fellow Latino comic: Greg said that Cheech was the only Mexican to ever *leave* America illegally—a reference to a rumor that Marin left the U.S. to avoid the Vietnam War draft.

Greg's success as a roaster was not only about content. His delivery played a crucial role. There are some exceptions, but in general a Greg Giraldo roast set went something like this . . .

It would begin with a short, offensive jab, directed at the roastmaster:

> *To Jason Alexander:* Thank you, Pillsbury Jewboy.

> *To Kathy Griffin:* Thank you, Tranny Bonaduce.

> *To Lisa Lampanelli:* Thank you very much, everybody. Lisa Lampanelli. Keep it going for that guy—wasn't he funny?

And it would end with a heartfelt declaration about the roastee, sprinkled with a joke to undercut the sentiment. Some examples:

> *To Bob Saget:* I'm done being mean, Bob. I've met you a bunch of times. You've always been hilarious and super cool, and everybody that knows you loves and respects you. Nobody ever has a bad thing to say about you, and that's particularly surprising, because you're Jewish, and you're obnoxious people.

> *To Pamela Anderson:* Now, I will say this, Pam, I'm seriously a giant fan of yours. We're going to make fun of you a lot here but to get to the level you've gotten is true genius. It really is absolute genius. People cannot help but love you. People can't help but love you. You've got unbelievable talent and you're America's sweetheart. You're a Canadian but those tits were made in America.

Greg adopted a consistent pace to his roasts. He didn't practice the timing. It came naturally. His cadence was nearly identical from roast to roast. Dave Diamond described it: "He's like, 'Well, this really worked here, so I'm going to use those exact same number of words with four different jokes and I just got to figure out what are the four things I can say about this person.'"

A typical strategy involved starting a joke directed at one person and switching unexpectedly to a different target. During a Courtney Love bit, Greg set up the joke by asking, "Courtney, what the hell happened to you? You were in a great band. You were a terrific singer."

Still looking at Courtney Love, Greg said, "And then your career dried up faster than Sarah Silverman's pussy around guys who can't help her in the business."

After so many roasts, though, Greg grappled to find new ways to push himself to keep his material original. He thought that many of the celebrities made for easy targets. The more obvious the target, the more he reached to make the joke complex. Greg shared in private: "The dais was often the same people or someone that was such a 'turd in a punchbowl,' like a sports figure or other non-comic, that it would be obvious and formulaic to make a small-dick joke, or a joke tinged with racism, so I work extra hard to avoid those traps."

Greg wanted the audience to think before reacting. If people laughed too fast, he considered it a failure because the joke was too obvious. Silence didn't bother him if it ended with a big payoff.

To outsiders, the roasts highlighted Greg's aggressive, confrontational comedy. However, behind the scenes, Greg was gracious and willing to assist others. Jesse Joyce experienced this first hand: "Greg really taught me a lot about how to treat younger comics because of how cool he was to me. He didn't have to do this at all, but he would loudly let everyone know that I was a big part of [the joke-writing process], which was super cool. He just did that for me. He didn't get anything out of it. If anything, it may have hurt his credibility."

Writer Robert Kurson praised Greg's roast performances: "I thought the guy was a genius. I thought he was brave . . . The way he stood up there and dished out the shit to celebrities much bigger than him—the guy's a nobody, at least at first—reminded me of the same kind of bravery it took to jump ship from a guaranteed future. And I always felt like I was watching a guy who was one of the bravest you'd meet."

Chapter 9
Comedy and the Road

How do you bare your soul through comedy in front of a bachelorette party that got 10 free tickets?
— Robert Kelly

In the 1980s, standup comedy in the United States boomed. More than 300 comedy clubs opened across the country from 1978 to 1988. This period ushered in some of the greats, including Eddie Murphy, Sam Kinison, and Steven Wright. Eager customers purchased tickets and satisfied their two-drink minimums. Seemingly anyone with enough confidence to perform could find a stage. Budding comedians quit their day jobs as a growing market allowed them to earn a living telling jokes. Clubs offered more than $500 a show to new acts and covered travel expenses. "It seemed very accessible," said Jim Gaffigan. "There were tons of people that were comedians."

But the standup comedy industry sputtered as the decade closed. Lines outside clubs got shorter. Customers spent less on entertainment. Venues ran fewer shows each week. Comedians clawed and scratched as opportunities dwindled and pay plummeted.

The New York comedy scene in the 1990s did not favor the timid. Even a legend like Rodney Dangerfield would get heckled at his own club. Comics who had flourished in the '80s did not want to risk their livelihoods to help new hopefuls advance. It took a brawler's mentality to make it. Audiences rarely forgave subpar comedy. Comics went toe to toe with discerning crowds. Gaffigan compared it to standing in front of a firing squad: "I know this sounds dramatic but it's true." No young comic could succeed without stage time.

Compared to most cities, New York offered more performance opportunities to aspiring comics. Different boroughs had their own cliques and codes. Greg and other hungry comedians traveled between Long Island and Manhattan to maximize stage time. Ted Alexandro recalled a division, even a rivalry, between the two scenes in the early 1990s: "It was more segregated: guys would do one or the other for the most part, and kind of look down on the other one. Greg and I being from Queens, we were very familiar with those places geographically, so that we both went back and forth between the scenes and benefited from that because there was good stage time to be had."

Greg bounced between Long Island venues like Governors and Chuckles to spots in Manhattan like Carolines and the Comic Strip. On some evenings, he and Gaffigan would trek for more than an hour to get to Chuckles. Showing up didn't guarantee stage time. The club's owner, John Trueson, would occasionally allow Greg to perform but make Gaffigan sit and watch.

Greg had a quick wit from the beginning and a knack for impressions. Audiences loved his stage presence. His charisma and crowd work helped him stand out. However, he needed repetition and practice to discover his voice. In his early years, Greg aimed to develop a persona like Brian Regan's—a hugely successful, clean, observational comic.

As time passed, Greg cultivated his own style. It focused on writing and refining. On stage, he delivered intelligent material in a controlled-rant fashion. Greg rarely played characters. He favored laughter over applause. Much of Greg's act involved his life experiences and current events. One of his signature jokes in the 1990s dealt with immigration. He took a non-obvious approach to the topic: "When was the last time an illegal alien stole your job? Oh, yeah, that dream job of the Chinese delivery man pedaling up Broadway delivering Chinese food for 40 cents an hour." Fans admired Greg's punchline-driven comedy. He read newspapers daily, searching for inspiration. Determining when to keep a joke versus when to give it up weighed heavily on him. He knew that adding a word or altering a line could transform an awful joke into a brilliant one. The crowd had the final say.

Comics respected Greg's approach. "I hung out with a bunch of guys who didn't carry notebooks. And then you'd see Greg writing jokes," said Robert Kelly. "He'd actually have notes and you're like, 'Oh, it's okay. That's what we do' . . . He was that guy, that cool dude who could have rested on his ego and confidence—but he also was that hard-working comedian that really tried to write funny shit."

Greg had a persistent drive to create new jokes. Although his mind worked faster than his hand could move, he wrote vigorously. Thoughts. Ideas. Bits. He scribbled them down in his barely legible handwriting.

Greg filled notebooks—some hardbound, others yellow legal pads—with pages of material. During a conversation, something funny would occur to him, and he would take out a notebook and jot it down. In the rare instances when he didn't have a notepad handy, he would write his thoughts on a napkin to be transferred later. Over time the musings resulted in an impressive collection of notebooks.

Greg's dedication led to more performance opportunities. One evening, Dave Attell canceled his headlining spot at Catch a Rising Star in Princeton, New Jersey, and Greg filled in for him. Greg's friend Ray Ellin was on the lineup, too.

That night Ellin watched Greg perform a long set. Greg took the stage with a headliner's confidence and annihilated. Punch line after punch line, he led the audience through a hilarious, invigorating experience. Ellin said: "We did two shows that night. He did 45 minutes each show, and he was excellent. He was just great."

Right after the shows finished, Ellin congratulated Greg on his inspired performances. "You were fantastic," Ellin said to Greg.

Unable to bask in his accomplishment, Greg deflected the compliment. Since his early days at open mics, Greg had admired Attell's brash, unadulterated comedy. Greg fixated on what he called "the genius of Dave Attell" and how he could never measure up to him.

Greg had an atypical view of genius. This subject prompted a debate one night in the front room of the Fat Black Pussycat, the sister bar of the Comedy Cellar. "Who's to say Michael Jordan isn't a genius?" Greg asked his friends at the table. "Look at the way he plays basketball. It's a form of genius."

"What are you talking about?" a comic interjected. "He's just bouncing a ball and who cares? He is not really using brain power."

Greg stood his ground and argued that genius took many forms, that it existed in artists, bankers, lawyers, and basketball players. "What Jordan does on the court and his instincts in doing it better than everybody else—there's a sort of brilliance in the way he plays the game," said Greg. "It's like a chess match."

While Greg's written material set the foundation for his standup sets, he often improvised and adjusted his act to the moment. He did not rely on crowd work as his comedy matured—he even called it a crutch. But he could take down a heckler with expert precision. Greg's standup wasn't usually confrontational. He didn't *look* to take people down. But when he did, it was effortless.

During a show at Stand Up NY on the Upper West Side, one unruly woman continually interrupted the comics.

All the performers were annoyed by her. Then Greg took the stage. She lit into him. He immediately responded with a four-minute rant about people believing too much in personal freedom and thinking the world revolves around them. "Society is crumbling as a result," said Greg.

And she was with him the whole time, yelling out, "Amen," and "Preach it," and "Yes," and doing everything Greg knew she would.

Stopping mid-sentence, Greg said to her: "And that is all about you." He faced her and shouted: "Everything you just agreed with is what you're violating right now." The intimate New York City crowd went nuts.

"It was brilliant," said an audience member who witnessed Greg's takedown. "I've never seen someone handle a terrible audience member better. Not just because he destroyed her, but he destroyed her in a way that everyone agreed with, even her . . . It was absolute artistry."

Greg offered the audience an honest look at his thoughts, feelings, and struggles. His onstage persona was like a magnified version of his offstage personality. Vulnerable. Sensitive. Acerbic. He came off as relatable and noncondescending.

"He was so real and honest and raw and so smart," said comedian Jessica Kirson. "He was very vulnerable. He was confident, but not intimidating; he was humble, he sold his jokes. He was strong; you knew not to fuck with him. His writing was brilliant. He was very likeable on and off stage. He just had it all."

By the end of the 1990s, Greg had established himself as a New York comedy stalwart. He performed regularly throughout the city, but he sought a home base. One club stood above the rest — the Comedy Cellar on Macdougal Street in Greenwich Village. The Cellar served as the unofficial headquarters of New York City comedy.

Founded in the early 1980s by Bill Grundfest, a writer and comedian, and Manny Dworman, a club manager from Israel, the establishment sat beneath a Middle Eastern restaurant called the Olive Tree. Many of the top East Coast standup comedians, such as Colin Quinn, Dave Attell, and Chris Rock, were regulars at this 150-seat basement club.

To get "passed" at the Comedy Cellar one had to impress Estee Adoram, an affable and unassuming woman who had moved to the United States from Israel. She began working at the Comedy Cellar in 1982 as a waitress. Adoram developed an eye for talent and soon became the Comedy Cellar's booker. She said, "I think that if somebody's going to be good, and I audition them, I start giving them spots — some exceptions. I'm not really highbrow . . . I understand what entertainment is. I don't want to make more of it than it actually is. It's not really a science. It's just common sense."

Adoram found Greg's style quirky and interesting. His intellect and ability to deliver lines with emotion and heart won her over. She loved him and his comedy. Adoram put him on heavy rotation.

The Comedy Cellar became Greg's workout room. When in town, he performed multiple sets on Fridays and Saturdays. During the week, he hit up two to three shows a night. On Sundays Greg often took a break from the stage to spend time with his family.

The Comedy Cellar offered Greg much more than a venue to develop his act. The club served as a support system. The waitstaff. Comedians. Management. They all grew close to Greg. The connection he shared with these people extended beyond setups and punch lines.

"He felt that I understood him," said Adoram, whom Greg affectionately called his comedy mother. "He was very open to me and I felt a great deal of warmth towards him. We trusted each other." Greg's kindheartedness stood out to her: "Just the way he relates to people, whether it was a smile, a hug, or if he'd tell you something, and you know it's confidential and you suddenly realize that he thinks a lot of you."

Greg developed a strong friendship with Manny and Noam Dworman. Manny Dworman, who passed away in late 2003, served as a fatherly mentor to many comics. He rarely shied away from sharing his opinions. He frequently clashed with comics over divisive issues. Manny earnestly wanted to help them learn. Certain confrontations grew so intense that Manny would purchase books such as Alan Dershowitz's *The Case for Israel* and give them to comics to help them educate themselves on world matters.

Manny and Greg, while close, would sometimes engage in heated arguments about politics, ideas, or beliefs. One skirmish escalated into a nasty verbal fight. The two friends shouted over each other. Their blood pressure rose, and they resolved nothing. Losing his cool in front of Manny weighed on Greg's conscience. He wanted to make amends. The next day Greg gave his own peace offering to Manny—a beautifully written apology letter in Greg's personal, informal style. Manny, so moved by Greg's gesture, made copies of the letter for safekeeping.

While Manny and Greg shared a tight bond, they were separated by a generation. Manny's son, Noam, on the other hand, served as a kindred spirit of sorts to Greg. Each had grown up in an immigrant home. They both loved music and excelled scholastically. Noam had also attended an Ivy League law school and, like Greg, grew disenchanted with the idea of law as a career. Manny demanded that his son take the bar. Noam passed it but never practiced law.

After graduating from the University of Pennsylvania Law School, Noam bypassed attorney life to pursue music. He reopened Café Wha? — a nightclub just steps from the Comedy Cellar. For almost 20 years, Noam entertained music fans as part of the house band. Between shows, Noam hung out at the Comedy Cellar. He would joke with Greg about working in law, but he knew Greg lacked the disposition to take orders. Greg stood out to Noam. "He was totally out of the ordinary," Noam said. "He was a step above anybody else."

Noam noticed Greg's gift. "Greg had every aspect that anybody in that industry would want," said Noam. "He was handsome, he was tall, he was athletic, he was smart, he was likeable, he was as quick-witted as Colin Quinn or any of the great comics, Seinfeld, or any of them. He was in their league and they knew it."

After sets, Greg walked upstairs to hang out at the Olive Tree restaurant. He would share food and discussion with comedians and Comedy Cellar staffers. Greg welcomed conversation. Still, he tended to be "on" after sets. Sparring wits was easy. Opening up was difficult. Offstage, Greg was more reticent about his feelings and concerns. On rare occasions, he would meet with Noam for dinner and drop his comedian pretenses. There were no jokes or spotlights — just two buddies hanging out.

"We had a conversation about my father one time, getting married and having kids," said Noam. "Those were my favorite times with him. Where I felt like we were just like friends."

The Olive Tree had an iconic table reserved exclusively for Comedy Cellar comedians. It acted as a de facto greenroom. The idea of the comedians' table began in the mid-1990s when Nick Di Paolo returned to New York. Di Paolo explained: "I just moved back from L.A. Literally, went down to the Comedy Cellar the night I got back. I was standing among all the bar patrons. I said to Manny, 'Can't you just reserve a table?' The next time I come in, sure enough, there's a table with a 'Reserved for Comedians' sign on it. That's why I love that guy. He was such a fan of comedians."

Conversations at the comedians' table were a precursor to *Tough Crowd*. Just as they did on the show, Greg and Patrice O'Neal clashed frequently. Di Paolo recalls one incident at the comedians' table: "Giraldo sounded like he had a few in him. I don't know what exactly they were feuding about but I was just sitting there, fucking smirking as I'm eating my Middle Eastern food. Just loving it. Patrice was keeping it cool, 'Fuck you, man' . . . Giraldo was like, 'Yeah, you fat fucker.' They're yelling across the restaurant . . . At that point, I think we had already started *Tough Crowd* so people knew who they were. I remember that night, seeing a different side of Giraldo."

Comedy Cellar regulars grew to appreciate Greg. Quinn, likely the most venerated New York comedian at the time, admired Greg's ability to build on his act. "Every time I saw him he had new material," said Quinn. "It was always stuff that was based on an issue that people were talking about, but it was a new bit or routine on it. He was the guy that would keep you honest."

Killing regularly at the Comedy Cellar helped cement Greg's reputation as a comic's comic. Robert Kelly said, "He'd go on stage and murder every night. Just murder. I had to follow him so many times. It'd be like, 'Fuck,' but it made me a better comic." Ted Alexandro christened Greg the "maestro" and blogged about how the city's most acclaimed comedians would put down their notebooks and stop arguing at the comics' table to watch Professor Giraldo take the stage. Alexandro wrote:

> *An exciting thing happens when one of these maestros takes the stage. The mundane rhythms of a comedy club are transformed. Comedians line the back of the room with childlike excitement in anticipation of something special. Even the waitstaff momentarily stops and becomes part of the audience. The fractured energies and scattered focus of the many are harnessed and fused into one energy – something inexplicably beautiful – in*

the hands of the maestros. When Greg Giraldo walked into a club, class was in session. I remember countless nights when I was filled with giddy excitement at the sight of Greg's arrival at a club. I'd take my place in the back and savor every moment of his performance. Greg possessed a very rare and special combination of gifts. He had a fierce intellect, a quick wit, a philosopher's insight and a sweet, goofy innocence that was infectious. The best comedians distill their essence with ease and you could see all of Greg up on stage every time he took the mic from the stand.

As a Comedy Cellar favorite, Greg connected with scores of entertainment executives. He would periodically fly to California to meet with them. But pitch meetings and pricey lunches held little appeal for Greg. Getting on stage and telling jokes made him feel at home.

The Laugh Factory on West Hollywood's Sunset Strip gave Greg a reprieve from show-business drudgery. Jamie Masada, a warmhearted Iranian immigrant, created the comedy venue in 1979. This club had a brighter, glitzier appearance than the Comedy Cellar. Comedians and fans loved the place. Greg endeared himself to Masada, who put Greg up regularly at the Laugh Factory.

During one show, comedian Rick Ducommun introduced Robin Williams, who jokingly tore into Masada.

"Hey, when are you going to lose your accent?" Williams inquired. "I bet you go home and speak perfect English."

Masada watched from the back of the club with Greg. Williams couldn't see Masada or Greg, who had performed earlier in the show. While Masada bit into a sandwich, Greg answered as if he were Masada, mimicking his Middle Eastern accent.

Greg tricked the Academy Award winner. For the next 25 minutes, the two comedians created some of the most hilarious improvised back-and-forth banter Masada had ever heard. At one point, Masada started choking, and Williams called out: "What's wrong? Are you choking on some pastrami from next door?"

"And I wasn't even fucking eating pastrami," Masada said, laughing. He loved their ability to improvise. "Robin was famous for it. Greg was not famous for it but he kept on with Robin," said Masada. "It was the most amazing thing I ever seen . . . Two of the most brilliant people sparring from— one off the stage, one on the stage . . . It was such a brilliant way he was going back and forth. It was amazing. The timing. Everything was amazing."

Williams eventually stopped his crowd work with "Masada" and returned to his more scripted act. Masada wanted Greg to stick around to let Robin Williams know that he wasn't the master-mind behind the exchange.

"Come on, Greg, I want to tell him that it was your voice, it wasn't me," Masada urged.

"See you later. I'm leaving. Bye," said Greg, who left before Williams finished.

Williams received a standing ovation, and afterward he said to Masada, "Man, I didn't know you're so brilliant." Masada didn't fess up.

"It was really the smartness of that night," Masada remembered about Greg's interaction with Robin Williams. "To come off his sleeve and start talking about stuff that he didn't practice . . . He didn't even say hello to Robin, say he was me, take a credit, nothing."

While Greg performed regularly at the Comedy Cellar, he also worked at several other New York comedy clubs. In 2000, Greg hung out at Gotham Comedy Club one evening. The club showcased several comics who performed eight- to 10-minute sets. Comedian Maryellen Hooper blew the roof off the place with an amazing set that fired up the crowd. Immediately after her performance, Patti Vasquez, a younger, less experienced comic, took the stage. She tagged some of her jokes by saying, "Am I right, ladies?" During her set, Greg left the club and didn't catch the rest of her act.

Then in 2003, Greg flew to Wisconsin to perform at Milwaukee's Comedy Cafe. He had no clue who his opening act would be. It turned out that Patti Vasquez would feature for her first time that weekend. She was nervous and remembered that Greg had walked out during her Gotham set a few years earlier. Now she had to entertain the packed Midwest crowd for almost half an hour.

Fortunately, in just a few years Vasquez had developed from a shy neophyte into a poised professional. She didn't beg the crowd for applause. She controlled the room. Greg loved how she joked about gender issues without appearing heavy-handed. Vasquez had found her footing and gained a new fan.

After her set, Greg was so impressed that he called her one of the top seven female comedians in the country. "It's such a specific number," said Vasquez on the distinction. She was flattered, and Greg's approval helped propel her career in comedy.

That weekend, however, Greg and Vasquez discussed more than just standup. They had to share an unkempt comedy condo, an accommodation that many clubs offer to out-of-town-performers when the managers don't want to pay for hotel rooms. Greg and Vasquez chatted about politics, his honeymoon, pretty much anything. His mind went nonstop. She noticed that nothing seemed to get past Greg. He was a keen observer of humanity and exhibited a strong sensitivity to injustice. Vasquez admired the knowledge and passion Greg had for so many subjects.

She also appreciated how he could relate to others. After the shows at the Comedy Cafe, Greg and Vasquez met up with a group of local bikers. After pounding several tequila shots, Greg and the Harley-Davidson enthusiasts exchanged tales of motorcycling mishaps. He had a great story about getting into an accident and seeing his whole life flash before his eyes. Greg held court, engaging the bikers with memories of working at Skadden and driving motorcycles. They loved him, and that weekend Vasquez, who would continue to open for Greg in the future, developed a deeper appreciation for his character.

"A lot of guys like him, they show up, they do the work, and they get out," said Vasquez. "They don't necessarily do anything to make the feature act feel welcome or important. He always did that for me."

Traveling from coast to coast, Greg made his living on the road. After dealing with crowded airports and checking in to chain hotels, Greg had to gear up for a hectic weekend of shows: one on Thursday, two on Friday and Saturday, then another on Sunday. Greg's friend Jessica Kirson knew the highs and lows of working the road: "It's very isolating. You're in hotels by yourself. You're not with a band . . . You're by yourself a lot of the time. So that's a very dangerous place to be for an addict."

Greg's Road Schedule

During the year and a half from March 2009 to September 2010, Greg traveled to at least 50 different spots all across the country, from New York to Los Angeles, and from Addison, Texas, to Bloomington, Minnesota

Additional bookings included:

- Larry the Cable Guy roast (March 1, 2009), Joan Rivers roast (July 26, 2009), and Hasselhoff roast (July 31–August 1, 2010), all in Los Angeles

- *Midlife Vices* special at the Union Square Theatre in New York City (June 17–18, 2009)

- *Can You Stump Greg Giraldo?* pilot in Los Angeles (December 15, 2009)

- European tour (arrived May 27, departed June 6, 2010): Amsterdam (May 28–29), Antwerp (June 1), Stockholm (June 3), Helsinki (June 4)

- Festival in Bonnaroo in Manchester, TN (June 12–14, 2010)

- Montreal Comedy Festival (July 9–11, 2010)

- *Last Comic Standing* in Los Angeles (August 8–10, 2010)

To help mitigate the dangers of touring, Greg's manager Rick Dorfman paired him with Jesse Joyce — a client of his who made a name for himself in New York after growing up in Pittsburgh. Joyce had stopped drinking on June 5, 2005 — 11 days after Greg's own commitment to sobriety. Joyce described Dorfman's thought process: "Rick was like, 'Hey, you need work. You are both chronic fuckups. It might be good if you guys did the road together.'"

The two comics developed a big-brother/little-brother rapport. They helped one another battle addiction. Greg mentored Joyce on the comedy business.

"I went from doing shitty B rooms . . . to doing great clubs," Joyce said. Joyce opened for Greg, whose headlining act went 60 to 90 minutes on most nights. Spur-of-the-moment reflections propelled Greg to come up with new bits. Joyce explained: "We would be on the road and on a Wednesday some goofy thing would happen, and we'd talk about it. We'd laugh about it at lunch, and then he would end up doing a version of it on stage. Then over the course of the week, I got to watch that turn into a really sharp bit."

Road life involved more than jokes and performances. Greg loved to visit local marinas to check out boats. It became a near obsession for him — he spoke passionately about specific features of the sea crafts. Joyce enjoyed driving boats but didn't share Greg's enthusiasm. "He would go off about how

171

great these dumb boats were," said Joyce on his visits with Greg to harbors.

While Greg offered guidance and mentorship to Joyce, he also provided his own style of juvenile hazing. Greg used swimming pools to razz Joyce at their various stops. If Joyce had an item he seemed overly attached to, Greg would throw it in the water. "He'd do it all the time," said Joyce. Before a show at the Tempe Improv, the club manager asked Greg and Joyce for headshots to help promote their show. Excited to be on the wall at the Improv, Joyce went out that day to get a professional photo of himself. "What do you got there?" Greg asked Joyce while lounging in a chair on the hotel balcony. Joyce handed Greg a file with his freshly printed headshot. After taking a glance, Greg threw it off the balcony into the swimming pool. At another hotel, Joyce rested his shoes on the bed. Before Joyce could react, Greg pulled them off and tossed them into the pool. "I would fall for it almost every week," said Joyce, who enjoyed the gag. "He would take something of mine, grab it, and throw it into the swimming pool." Joyce added: "It really cracked me up because it was a real ball-busty thing that I would fall for all the time."

After shows, Greg and Joyce often went to movie theaters to pass the time and avoid trouble. Like many real-life brothers, Joyce and Greg had occasional disagreements. One source of conflict involved Greg's place in comedy's pecking order: he was annoyed that other comedians were more successful than he was. Joyce noticed a common theme to Greg's frustration: "We'd be on the road and he would see that someone like Pablo Francisco would be doing a theater in town. Greg would be the special event at the Improv, but Gaffigan or Pablo or somebody would be doing the theater. We'd pass a billboard and he'd be like, 'What do you gotta do to do a fuckin' theater?'" As an up-and-coming comedian, Joyce felt insulted by Greg's displeasure with his status in comedy. Greg was where Joyce hoped to end up. Listening to Greg complain about his perceived lack of stature annoyed Joyce—but it didn't surprise him. "As a comic, I completely understand it," said Joyce. "It's this never-ending thing." Greg lamented that the exposure he received early on—a network sitcom and national attention—may have actually hurt his career in later years.

Joe Schrank, who accompanied Greg on several road shows later in his career, believed Greg preferred humble rooms to ritzy auditoriums. "Greg did grimy comedy club after grimy comedy club and sabotaged the opportunities to get off the road," Schrank said. "He wanted to be in those places, staying at the fucking Marriott doing three shows on Saturday night."

Fans and radio hosts treated Greg like a local celebrity. The thrill of performing caused certain occupational hazards for Greg. "I'm feeling so energized, especially if I had a really good night," Greg said about his state of mind after a set. "My heart is racing, my adrenaline's pumping . . . I don't want to go home. I don't even want to go to sleep. I'm feeling like a million dollars up on that stage. And it is just hard to let go of that."

Inevitably, someone would ask Greg, "Where are you partying?" These invitations created too many opportunities for misadventures. As Greg spent more time on tour, he took extra precautions to avoid the traps of relapse. Sober companions like Joyce and Schrank helped distract him from common pitfalls.

While large theaters may have appealed to Greg's ego, the more intimate comedy clubs offered him a better environment to connect with crowds. He delivered material as if he were in a conversation with the audience. In his later years, Greg addressed the growing acceptance of gay marriage while alluding to his own marital struggles. One of Greg's more popular joke series involved the sanctity of traditional unions. Greg shared with the audience: "First of all, it's certainly not sacred. And second of all, if a man wants to marry another man, good luck with it."

After a brief silence, Greg added, "You don't choose whether you're gay or not. You are what you are."

And then: "How do you discriminate against someone for being who they are? I don't *choose* to be attracted to women. I happen to be attracted to women — it sucks."

Greg resumed: "That means every 10 years or so, I have to give all my shit away and start from scratch," an allusion to his two ill-fated marriages.

After that punch line, Greg said: "There is a level of gayness that seems to be on purpose. At that point, it's probably okay to laugh . . . I think."

Greg continued: "I was on a plane the other day, and the flight attendant — a guy — with the cart was like" — altering his voice to a nasal, effeminate effect, Greg exclaimed — "Snaaaacks, would you like snacks, sir?"

Then Greg remarked in his own voice, "That's got to be a choice. You could definitely scale that back some."

Greg added, "If you have to say *snacks* over and over again, it would make anyone sound pretty over-the-top. This guy had to push the cart and say it 400 times."

Going back to the effeminate voice, Greg simulated a tired flight steward: "Snacks, sir, for you a snaaack. Snack for you, ma'am? Snack. Snack. Snaaaack. Let me suck your dick, sir. Pleeeease let me suck your dick, just the tip."

Waiting for the laughter to die down, Greg said in character, "No? Then snaaaacks."

He then offered a nuanced take on gay marriage: "I have three sons, and somebody asked me if I'd care if one of my sons was gay."

175

Greg answers, "How gay? If one of them turns out to be gay and wants to marry a dude, that should be his right. And I'd support that."

The audience offered stately applause to signify that it was on the same page as Greg on this issue. Not one to pander to a crowd, he moved on: "But if I get on an airplane and my son gets behind me and goes 'Snaaaacks, snack, Dad? Snaaaaacks,' he could dial that down a little, tiny bit, that's all I'm saying."

"If he wants to bring his new husband to Thanksgiving dinner, great, but if they start fisting the turkey . . . I'm kidding, of course, I wouldn't give a shit if one of my sons was gay—I have two normal ones."

"I have two normal, decent ones with a shot of getting into heaven."

Circling back to his fatherhood material, Greg discussed how people would tell him that they knew what it was like to have children because they had dogs. His reply: "Nobody has a dog because you were too drunk to pull out."

Greg worked with other opening acts besides Joyce. One such comic was Floridian Patrick Melton, who met Greg at the Orlando Improv during St. Patrick's Day weekend in 2007. Melton, a sharp-witted comic with an imposing six-foot-five frame, had started in comedy just five years before connecting with Greg. In spite of their outward differences, Greg and Melton shared some common ground. Both comedians had lost their fathers to esophageal cancer, Greg's in 2002, and both had bits about a famous pop star's wardrobe malfunction. Melton remembered that weekend fondly.

After the emcee introduced Melton, he lumbered onstage and launched into his set. Melton commented on the recent big news — Britney Spears had flashed her crotch while exiting a limousine.

"'Boo, Britney Spears's vagina,'" Melton said to the packed Orlando crowd. "Everybody was going crazy about it."

"I'd been dreaming about this since the '90s," added Melton. "I expected it to be a lot better than it was. I didn't want a C-section scar. I expected it to be magical. Chocolate waterfalls and rainbows, and everybody gets free lottery tickets."

Greg began his set with his own Britney Spears joke — commenting on how amazing it was to see her vagina. Then, breaking routine, Greg stopped and said, "I can't do this bit. Patrick's was so much better."

Greg dropped the joke and moved on with his act. About 45 minutes later, Greg exited the stage and immediately complimented Melton on his Britney Spears joke.

"I just fucking melted," said Melton. "This guy had every right to be a bitter dick to me . . . I still regard it as one of the most cherished comments from a comedian."

That weekend Greg took Melton out for lunch. They hung out with St. Patrick's Day partiers and talked comedy. Greg supported Melton's comedic aspirations and offered encouragement. He suggested that Melton trust his instincts.

"You're a funny person," Greg told Melton as they discussed how much to rework punch lines. "So whatever line popped into your head is probably a funny line, so go with that."

Greg performed with Melton on several more weekends in Florida over the next two years. Greg's sincerity in helping a near-stranger impressed Melton. "I never once felt any kind of attitude, bitterness, jealousy, weird headliner angst," Melton said.

Comedy pundits celebrated Greg's live shows. Dylan Gadino, founder of Laughspin.com (formerly known as *Punchline Magazine*) called Greg's performances cathartic: "I laughed my ass off, I thought a lot, I got anger out, I got frustration out." Greg was one of the few comedians who "dragged me through the wringer, and I mean that in a good way."

Greg's humor had an element of surprise. Ted Alexandro appreciated that Greg's material kept him guessing. "The only thing consistent is that he's going to be funny," said Alexandro.

Journalist Sean McCarthy first saw Greg perform at the Improv in Tempe, Arizona, and he never forgot it. "I was just blown away," McCarthy said. "He had this way of being the smartest guy in a theater of 400 people without making anyone in the audience feel like he was talking down to you. He never sounded pretentious. He never sounded self-righteous. He was just right."

He left such an impression on audiences that Jamie Masada bestowed on Greg a distinction possibly more prestigious than any Ivy League degree:

> *He got from me a title of Doctor of the Soul . . . He really was one of those comedians, like Rodney Dangerfield . . . George Carlin . . . Richard Pryor . . . Robin Williams . . . If you're like, "I'm going on the stage because So-and-So made millions" . . . fuck you, you're not going to ever make it. But if you go on the stage to make people laugh, you're one of the chosen person to become a Doctor of the Soul — to help people's soul — then you deserve to go on the stage . . . Greg Giraldo, he was one of the smartest, brilliant comedians, and he earned from me a Doctor of the Soul.*

Chapter 10
Addiction

Being on stage is therapeutic. It's not therapy, but it is definitely therapeutic.

— Dr. Ildiko Tabori

Matt Paroly, Greg's housemate from Harvard Law School, experienced two distinctly different standup performances from Greg. The first took place in the early 2000s at the Meadow Brook Amphitheatre, an impressive venue in Rochester, Michigan. Once Paroly had received word that his old law school buddy was performing near him, he grew excited. He told his friends, bought tickets, rented a bus, and joined thousands of Giraldo fans at the big outdoor concert hall. They were not disappointed — they laughed so hard they could barely breathe. This was Greg at his best. He gave an inspired performance. Greg dazzled the audience with his finely honed bits. To this Michigan crowd, Greg was adored as much as any celebrity. They loved him.

Still energized from the show, Paroly and his friends met up with Greg at a large sports bar about 20 minutes away from the amphitheater. It could not have been a better reunion. Hundreds of patrons threw back pitchers of beer, ate too many hot wings, and enjoyed the evening. Excitement grew when Greg arrived. "You were so funny," said a pleasantly buzzed woman. All sorts of people approached

Greg. He signed autographs, received praise from fans, fended off groupies. He loved it.

Just a few years later though, in 2005, Paroly had a profoundly different experience. Greg was playing at the Comedy Castle in Royal Oak, about 15 miles south of where Paroly lived. He knew that something had changed with Greg. In the days leading up to the show, Paroly received several messages from Greg in which he asked for painkillers, uppers, downers — seemingly anything to alter his consciousness. But Paroly had nothing to satisfy Greg's requests.

Paroly went to the show anyway. This time Greg bombed. He looked like a zombie, telling rambling stories and struggling to entertain the audience. The evening ended with Greg shouting at some unruly customers after the show. The yelling and screaming grew so intense that the club's bouncers escorted Greg out of the building.

"Wow, that's a different guy," said Paroly's friend, who had attended Greg's earlier show in Rochester. They had witnessed a dramatic change in Greg.

Especially in his later years, Greg was incredibly candid about his substance abuse. He discussed it in interviews and onstage. He knew that drinking and taking drugs didn't make him funnier. He referred to alcohol and drugs as the "medicine to fix what's wrong" and mentioned that abusing them couldn't work because it failed to address the root psycho-logical cause of the distress.

In an extended interview on the *Opie and Anthony* radio show in May 2009, Greg was extraordinarily forthright about his addiction. He joined Jim Norton and Patrice O'Neal in studio, where they talked openly about drinking and drug abuse. Jay Mohr called the show to offer his perspective on the subject.

Greg acknowledged that he had been separated from his wife for the past six months, and affirmed that he was sober. "I'm good now," said Greg. "I had my little substance issues and I went off the rails again for a while, but now it's all back, man, back in black." He talked about his penchant to over-drink and the impact it had on his comedy: "It makes you much less funny, much less creative. Everything. It's a total fucking self-destructive nightmare."

Greg discussed how he would trick himself into thinking he needed to drink to prepare for his shows. He mentioned that for years he would drink every time he went onstage and he enjoyed it. Eventually, he had to end that habit. He would stop drinking for several months, but then he would start again and initially feel looser, funnier. Greg feared that sobriety would make him less funny, but he then saw that it had the opposite effect.

He reached the final straw. Half-jokingly, he said that he was onstage and noticed a look of horror on a compassionate face in the crowd. At that point, he knew he had to change.

During the radio show, the comedians swapped several stories about drugs and alcohol. Greg brought up a time when his drug-induced partying had caused paranoia and hallucinations. He ended up lying in a hotel room where he felt like he was being attacked by robotic creatures with laser beams for eyes.

He went on to discuss being on a flight to a college gig where he thought everybody around him was an agent out to get him. "And then there was this Indian woman sleeping behind me, and I kept looking between . . . the seats . . . I go, 'They're so clever to put a woman pretending to sleep behind me,'" Greg said. "She's pretending to sleep but she's listening the whole time."

Apparently, the passengers noticed Greg's erratic behavior. Once the plane landed, a group of police officers met him outside the gate. He had calmed himself enough to appear coherent. The cops said they had cause to arrest him, but Greg told them he hoped they wouldn't. They relented and left him alone.

Mohr brought up his own tales of substance abuse. He mentioned that a bottle of Nyquil caused him to fall off the wagon. Greg, who said he used to be skeptical of accidental relapses, joked about being at a dentist's office and angling to get more nitrous oxide while they worked on his teeth.

The discussion shifted back to comedy. Mohr thanked Greg for helping him book more high-paying corporate shows. According to Mohr, Greg had upset some people at Reebok during a company event. Greg had allegedly called a woman a "cunt" during his performance, and the company elected not to book him again. The next year Reebok hired Mohr. "Thanks for the 50 G's," said Mohr. This story sparked more dialogue on the effects that drug use can have on a career. Greg mentioned that he could justify getting fewer "whorish corporate gigs" by telling himself that he didn't want to do them in the first place. He explained that addicts can rationalize anything until they lose what they care about the most.

The show's participants took a serious tone in their conversation with Greg. They listened with apparent suspicion as Greg said he could manage to have a few drinks of wine while on dates, but that his addiction problems were behind him. They recognized the gravity of substance abuse and how difficult it was to control. Norton, who had quit drinking in 1987, affirmed many of Greg's points and mentioned that alcohol created an illusion. It blocked creativity. It wrecked everything.

Greg's assessment of his current circumstance did not inspire much confidence. "I think that I'm done," he said. "But God knows."

Norton and Greg examined various roadblocks to sobriety. "People know what they have to do," said Norton. "They either want to do it or they don't." Greg responded by saying that the triggers to relapse can be subtle and that getting sober tended to be harder for analytical people, those who overthought things. They looked for loopholes. "If we can pray to God to help us get sober, why can't we form a group to pray to God for moderate drinking?" asked Greg.

Greg speculated about the fundamental reasons for his tendency toward addiction. A motivating factor was the pressure he felt to do things to gratify others: "I was so fucking busy being the good kid and trying to do things I didn't want to." He brought up going to law school, trying to please his parents, getting married.

Greg sought a remedy for his distress. He said, "I'm not that comfortable in my skin in real life. Onstage, I could get a little buzzed, and I could be the guy I wanted to be my whole life. Now I'm loose and cool and comfortable and relaxed and not self-conscious . . . I always felt weird. I always felt different. And I still do now to this day. I'm standing here. Even you guys, even the crew and these guys. I'm always on the periphery of everything. I'm always the outsider. You know it doesn't matter. And people tell me, 'But people like you. You're normal.' But I never felt that way, never. Soon as I got fucked up, it was like, 'Hey, everybody, now I'm one of you. I'm normal.'"

Throughout the *Opie and Anthony* episode, Patrice O'Neal showed concern for Greg. He was legitimately surprised to learn the extent of Greg's substance abuse. O'Neal referred to Greg as a "straitlaced" influence who helped keep things together on *Tough Crowd.* He wanted to help Greg and not play to the listeners. "I want to be his real friend on this," said O'Neal. "I don't want to be his radio friend."

Alcoholism affects many, and Greg's feelings were likely shared by millions. Despite its prevalence, alcoholism is often under-discussed and stigmatized. "It's extremely common," said Dr. Lyndsay Merrill. "It's just people don't talk about it." In her treatment of substance abuse sufferers, Dr. Merrill has experienced what patients go through during withdrawal. That pain is so intense that they look for anything to make it go away. Most people with severe addiction will relapse several times before they finally get clean, if they ever get clean at all.

Greg discussed his addiction with several of those close to him. Noam Dworman was aware of Greg's condition but didn't know its magnitude. "I guess I was naïve," said Dworman. "I didn't realize how overwhelming it was." However, many had already noticed its signs. Estee Adoram recalled an incident when Greg punched a wall at the Comedy Cellar and fell to the floor. "It was very apparent that he was suffering," said Adoram, who feared

Greg's condition was worsening. "I tried to hide it from other people but then, you can't hide something like that. Everybody knew."

Greg's outbursts were not limited to the Comedy Cellar. During a show at the Gotham Comedy Club, Greg became irate with Jim Gaffigan for doing a guest set on the same night when *he* was performing. The reaction was out of character for Greg. Gaffigan didn't think his own appearance was a big deal—but Greg considered it upstaging. Gotham's co-owner, Chris Mazzilli, told Gaffigan that Greg had been going through some tough stuff. A few months later Mazzilli called Gaffigan to ask if he could substitute for Greg, who had punched the wall and appeared to have broken his hand.

Greg's binges tended to start with alcohol and escalate to harder substances. A confidant said: "He would start drinking and then he'd go into a spiral of . . . trying to go up and down and just normalize, and then he'd do a come-down and wake up and then start from scratch, building his life again. Fixing the wreck that he created."

These episodes were not happy times for him. He was not out with friends socializing. He'd do it alone or at someone's house—he'd go into a dark place.

Comedian Dom Irrera also witnessed Greg's drug use, and attributed it partly to Greg's personality: "Greg was the kind of guy that couldn't do anything unless it was to excess." Irrera, who is more than 15 years older than Greg, hated to see his younger friend hurt himself. It was "a point of contention" between them, Irrera said, something that he worried about a lot. "Can't you just get high?" he asked Greg. "Why you got to get to the point where you're going to put your life in danger?"

Greg's addiction had tangible effects on his career. He once failed to appear for a part he had on Comedy Central because he was not in the right condition to perform. On another occasion, Greg drank at an airport bar for so long that he missed his flight. As a result, he didn't make his call time for a role on an NBC show. The network's personnel reworked the show's schedule to shoot Greg's part the next day. Twenty-four hours passed, and, again, Greg did not show.

Greg Helping Others in Need

Greg and I went to the same elementary school in Auburndale, Queens. He was over 10 years older than me, but where we met was at the Caron Treatment Facility in 2008. In 2008 I was having a benefit for a man that was terminally ill and even though Greg was in early recovery dealing with his own struggles, he was willing to help out. He was a light that shined in the dark and brought joy and laughter to me and others. He was a good man.

–Anonymous

Greg tried doggedly to get sober. He had a pattern during adulthood—several months of sobriety followed by a brief relapse. He had sober friends and coaches to assist him. He also tried rehab. Nothing seemed to work. Part of the impediment was that Greg did not completely buy into the philosophy of the Alcoholics Anonymous program. He attended meetings but didn't always identify with the people and the message. He didn't follow all the mantras and the steps. He disliked viewing alcoholism as an illness.

Jessica Kirson said, "He just couldn't get it. I mean, he couldn't stick to it. He couldn't commit to the program and he just was suffering."

Joe Schrank, a sober companion and close friend of Greg, has dedicated much of his adult life to assisting those suffering from substance abuse. He believed that Greg was not an ideal candidate for total abstinence and strict adherence to a 12-step program. "He really had a hard time in AA, a very hard time connecting with people," said Schrank. "He had a very hard time with people who would tell him, 'You didn't do this and you didn't do that and you didn't do a fourth step. That's your problem. You didn't read the big book.' He was way too intelligent and intellectual to really connect with blue-collar people. He liked blue-collar people. Being a kid from Queens, he definitely liked them, but they couldn't assume a leadership role for him."

Greg worked to curb his substance abuse. Not known as a frequent partier, he longed to enjoy a drink in moderation. And for much of his adulthood, Greg abstained from his vices. In his later days especially, he made a concerted effort to live more healthily. He exercised regularly and even began to flirt with veganism. But the temptations were always there.

Comedy to Those in Need

Saranne Rothberg, the founder of the Comedy Cures Foundation, recalls her experience of Greg Giraldo:

I had just beaten stage IV cancer the first time I saw Greg Giraldo perform live. For years, I had heard from Greg's peers about his comic prowess, "He's a genius," and "Greg's the Ivy League comic." Many comics would joke about Greg's Harvard pedigree, but they would also tell me that Greg was "a comic's comic." So when Greg Giraldo walked on stage at the re-opening of the New York Improv,* I paid attention; and then I laughed and I laughed hard. There were several comedy heavyweights who performed there that opening show but the night belonged to Greg Giraldo. He not only killed; he annihilated all of us. I could not wait to meet Greg, and I immediately went over to introduce myself and congratulate him on his fantastic set. I told him that he had "blown me away."

I shared with Greg that I was a stage IV survivor and that I had started the Comedy Cures Foundation from my chemo chair in 1999. Greg immediately offered to help with our ComedyCures.org mission to bring comedy to kids and adults living with illness, depression, trauma, and disabilities. Our paths crossed several more times but I will always remember that stellar performance and his instant compassion—unexpected from one of the heavyweight Friars Club roast masters, but so much about Greg was unexpected.

The New York Improv was under a new hybrid partnership at that opening and then later was renamed the Broadway Comedy Club.

Schrank supported Greg's efforts to get healthier. The two lived together after Greg's separation. According to Schrank: "We both felt overwhelmed and insecure in our roles as providers and fathers. While we were going through simultaneous divorces, the two of us became roommates and were consumed by the fear that we'd end up living in my tiny West Village apartment forever. It became like a bizarre bipolar, alcoholic version of *The Odd Couple*."

When Greg roomed with Schrank, he worked to improve his physical fitness. Still, he would try to indulge his sweet tooth on occasion. He wanted to treat himself with candies and cookies. But Greg had an unorthodox technique to stop himself from eating these snacks. He would jump on his bag of Oreos, crushing them into a sandy consistency. To prevent any further temptation to eat them, Greg urinated on the Oreos, too. "That's literally the only way that he could stop himself," said Schrank. "Piss on your bag of cocaine or your Xanax or whatever the fuck."

Schrank was upset about the shame and stigma of addiction. He said, "People who die of addiction or mental illness get, 'What the fuck is wrong with them?' . . . The more we learn about it, the more we know that it's centered in the brain." Dr. Merrill added that medical research supports the claim that alcoholism has a genetic component. "So we assume that's the case with other substances as well," said Dr. Merrill. "And we do think of substance abuse as also a brain disorder."

When Barack Obama was first elected in 2008, ABC News interviewed Oprah Winfrey. Greg and Schrank watched the television as Winfrey mentioned that she had encouraged several residents of a local drug rehab center to vote for Obama. Winfrey mentioned that many of the women had been in detox for less than a week. Then she said, "Okay, that's good, that's sober enough . . . and I thought, *Listen, we will even take the drug addict vote. We will even do that.*" Schrank, shocked by what he heard, thought to himself, *What the fuck kind of thing is that to say?* Greg responded with a harsh joke: "Oprah, how did you stop chewing long enough to shame us drug addicts?"

Greg's profession made staying sober particularly difficult. Comedians are often alone with easy access to alcohol and drugs. Nick Di Paolo said, "I remember when we did the Pam Anderson roast. He had just quit drinking like a month earlier. We flew out together and we checked into the hotel. We go to his room first and we open the door and there's a huge basket, a gift basket that Comedy Central sent all us comedians. Of course it was all booze. It was Wild Turkey. He just picked it up and handed it to me. He goes, 'Get this out of my room.' He goes, 'What are they, trying to fuckin' kill me?'"

Comedian Robert Kelly, who "got sober young," talked about the pressure of the job and how hard it is to stay sober:

> *Nobody really enjoys this fucking comedy gig. Dude, okay, you have a beautiful family and you never get to see them. You're on the road and you're worried about ticket sales and it's an up and down and you feel good. You feel like shit. You feel good. You feel like shit. You're alone. You can't do anything. You can't have sex with anybody. You can't smoke anything. You can't drink anything. You can't snort anything. You're not supposed to eat shitty because you're going to*

be on TV and so you got to look good. There's nothing, so you basically have to be some sort of superhero. And how do you deal with that without some type of spirituality or foundation around you that can help you, you can talk to? Because we're headline comedians. We're alone.

Even when Greg wasn't on the road, he encountered challenges that made staying sober difficult. The root causes of addiction didn't stop when the shows ended. Jay Mohr said that the combination of thinking like a comedian, being smart, but also being an addict was very difficult: "I wouldn't want to walk around with that brain. It's hard enough to just walk around as a comic with dopes. When that demon, or that disease crawls back into your skin, that's tough . . . You have to get high at the right time. Make sure you don't drink this much before this show and in between, make sure you only do this, and it's just a countdown. It's a stopwatch until something terrible happens."

Feelings of alienation and mental distress are common for many comedians. After three comics committed suicide in a relatively short time span, the Laugh Factory hired a resident psychologist. One of the comedians was Drake Sather—a wryly funny performer who wrote *Zoolander*. He shot himself to death on March 3, 2004, at age 44.

Greg's Tattoos

Greg had two tattoos, each done at different times in his life. His first one, on his right biceps, memorialized his wedding day with MaryAnn McAlpin: "MaryAnn 1-23-99." He briefly discusses the tattoo on the A&E special *Tattoo Fixation* in 2006, where he jokes: "It's my wife's name and the day we were married, unless I'm with a hooker, and then it's the day that my daughter was born."

Greg's other tattoo is on his left forearm. This one was done during his later years when he changed his hair and his clothes to give himself a more rock 'n' roll look.

He told Dylan Gadino in an interview: "It represents a lot of things to me that are not interesting to anybody else. Basically, it was a moment where I thought I was going to radically change my life for good, and that didn't necessarily play out that way."

The change that Greg is referring to is his effort to control his drinking and drug-taking, reflected in the "525" of the tattoo which referred to May 25, 2005, the first day of his sobriety. But he was elusive about the meaning of that date as well: "It doesn't mean any one date. . . And there's a series of rings here that means something I don't remember."

There was Freddy Soto—a former driver for Richard Pryor. Laugh Factory owner Jamie Masada had encouraged Soto to try standup.

One night Soto took the stage at a 10 p.m. Laugh Factory show. He was hilarious. The crowd gave him a standing ovation. Soon Soto got a job at the Comedy Store about a half-mile west of the Laugh Factory on Sunset. He became one of Masada's favorite comedians. In 2005, Soto met up with Masada in the lobby of the Laugh Factory. There, Soto kissed Masada on the back of his neck and thanked him for encouraging him to take up standup comedy. About a week later, Soto committed suicide.

There was also Richard Jeni—a widely respected comic who achieved crossover success in film and television. Masada remembers an evening in early March 2007:

> I look around. It's Richard. I said, "Richard, what's going on?" "Nothing, man. I just want to tell you how much I love you, man. I really love you, man." That's affected me. I said, "Richard, I love you too. Give me a hug." I gave him a hug. He couldn't hug me. Somehow, his hand was just like a wooden—he couldn't put an arm around you to hug you . . . I start going. He said, "Jamie, I love you." It just got to me. I turned around. I said, "Richard." I jokingly, jokingly—"You didn't become one of those fruitcake or something like that?" I start joking around with him. He

> *looked at me and said, "No, I really love you, man." Two days later, Saturday, I get a phone call from his girlfriend that he put a gun in his mouth and blow himself up.*

Dr. Ildiko Tabori, the in-house psychologist that Masada hired, has a unique perspective on the range of issues that impact comedians. She is a licensed clinical psychologist specializing in matters of the brain and behavior.

According to Dr. Tabori, addiction is not an independent affliction, unrelated to the rest of a person's life. It is a coping mechanism. Happy people don't abuse drugs. "If things are going great in your life, you're not going to be smoking crack," said Dr. Tabori. "Substance abuse does not exist in a vacuum."

Dr. Tabori followed Greg's career, and she noticed that the subject matter of his material seemed to reflect his mental state. "You can see him starting in a really great, positive place and being really successful," she said, "and then things went awry. I don't know what was necessarily going on in his personal life but you can see it in his comedy where he started to get really, really angry on stage, and it was dramatic, the difference."

She surmised that most of Greg's mental struggles didn't *start* with drug use. "He was doing drugs *because* he was sad and depressed," said Dr. Tabori.

She also speculated that a desire to perform often has more to do with low self-esteem than confidence. Some comedians view the stage as the only place where they can get attention. "And if they're not center stage, they're not comfortable and they start feeling those self-doubts," said Dr. Tabori. "Somebody who is feeling secure doesn't always need to be the center of attention."

When it came to addressing the causes of his angst, Greg thought initially that alcohol and drugs helped him cope. He said: "I'm actually fixing my problem. I'm treating my illness." Then he quickly learned that this approach didn't work. "And then you try to stop, and not drink or anything, and all of a sudden that illness is still there with no medicine," Greg said. "It gets fucking worse and worse and worse—until you address what's wrong with you, then you're going to keep picking up and going back down that path."

Although he worked to address what was wrong, Greg's sobriety did not last. In his later years, the same back-and-forth pattern continued. He had periods when he was clean and sober for several months, but others when he was again bingeing on drugs and alcohol.

Chapter 11
Comic Standing

You've got to seize whatever opportunity you can while keeping true to your comedy . . . Do whatever it takes to increase exposure to your standup. That's what he was thinking.

—J-L Cauvin

After nearly 20 years as a comedian, Greg's recognition grew and he became a bigger name in the comedy world. Perhaps his most visible role occurred in 2010 as a judge on NBC's *Last Comic Standing*. This show exposed Greg to a national audience.

Last Comic Standing first aired in 2003 and followed the model of several reality television shows. Fame seekers from across the country auditioned for 10 spots. A group of bold and contrasting personalities competed for a prize while living under the same roof. Cameras caught the bickering and backstabbing. There were challenges, including how to promote shows, and street performing to tourists. It mixed standup comedy with on-camera posturing. The winner earned a cash prize, a development deal, and other accolades. It was the perfect show for grizzled comedians to love to hate.

Greg's first affiliation with *Last Comic Standing* was as a guest performer. Here's an excerpt from one of his sets. Some of the material had been used from his earlier days in comedy and on the DVD *Midlife Vices:*

> *I watched a show the other day on food addiction, a special on food addiction, and they had all these people on there complaining about their food addiction. One woman was super passionate. She was like, "I'm a food addict. I'm addicted to food. It's an addiction. It's a disease. It's an addiction, just like alcoholism or drug addiction." Yeah, just like alcoholism or drug addiction? How come then when a wife kicks you out of the house for being a drunk or a drug addict, she's, you know, a big hero. But if you kick her out for fattening up a little bit, you know, that's not quite as cool, right? Maybe you're just trying to help her hit rock bottom. "Is that powdered sugar on your shirt? Have you been eating? Oh my god, you are stuffed in front of the kids."*

The show changed formats in subsequent seasons. In 2004, NBC pulled the plug on it and then brought it back in 2006. It went off the air in 2009.

2010 appeared to be a make-or-break year for *Last Comic Standing.* The show's producers wanted Greg to be a judge, but Greg mulled over the offer with trepidation. The idea of judging other comedians caused an intense conflict for him. He thought, *Who the fuck am I to sit there and judge other comics?*

He said, "I don't want to be an asshole and tell somebody they had a bad set because they really did have a bad set or because I'm told by a producer to do so."

Greg had other concerns about the opportunity. He discussed the offer with Ted Alexandro, who thought Greg was trying to make a case for something he didn't want to do. Greg lamented: "We're all just in the circus. You've got to work. There's no delineating what is good or what is bad. It's a job, and we're all just trying to make a living."

The lure of steady pay appealed to Greg. He took the gig but on his own terms. He explained, "I'm not going to sit here and be the bad guy and be an asshole to the comedy community because I got a deal to be on a TV show."

Greg joined the judging panel with comedians Natasha Leggero and Andy Kindler. Kindler was initially hesitant to participate in the show. But he later called *Last Comic Standing* one of his greatest experiences because it got him closer to Greg. "He had such a sweetness to him," said Kindler. "I've rarely seen it in many people — let alone comics."

Leggero remembered that Greg didn't say much when they first met, but that his true character — "super intelligent, super funny, really sweet" — came out when they started to work together. The three judges built a natural chemistry that came through on camera.

"We could laugh at each other while sitting next to each other; very rarely can comics do that," Kindler said. "[Greg] liked other comics to be funny . . . He loved it, and I think we hit it off, too."

Veteran comedians, including Kirk Fox, Laurie Kilmartin, and David Feldman, auditioned for the first episode in L.A. along with several less-established comics.

Greg offered kindness and encouragement to the show's performers. Leggero said: "Greg seemed to always really want them to make sure they had a fair shot and sometimes, if I thought someone was bad and I had a funny quip about it, I would just kind of shout it out. And Greg, he would be thoughtful and be like, 'Well, do you want to have another shot at this, sir? Would you like to do another few minutes?' He was just really kind to the people in a way that I wasn't at that point."

Greg's presence on *Last Comic Standing* increased the show's cachet. "I feel like having Greg Giraldo on even for a season of *Last Comic Standing* says, 'Hey, we are legitimate in our appreciation of standup,'" said contestant J-L Cauvin.

One of the season's longer-lasting contestants, Myq Kaplan, added: "I think he was one of the most respected comedians, period, and so he was certainly one of the most respected judges that did grace the stage of that show. I think he added credibility and a level of comedy prestige to it."

Greg offered his feedback in a soft, constructive manner. His warmth and sincerity were evident to the live audience.

Donna Moore-sturgill, a comedy aficionado from Rhode Island, attended several tapings of *Last Comic Standing* with her teenage daughter. They sat far away from Greg in the rafters at the NBC studio, but he made a lasting impact on them.

She noticed that Greg seemed to take every possible opportunity to provide feedback to each contestant. He did so with reverence and a deeply rooted desire to help.

"Hell, even 'from the cheap seats' *we got it*," Moore-sturgill said. "I felt like I really 'heard' him. He was that good at connecting — absolutely no doubt the best on that panel."

Comedians vied for Greg's approval — especially J-L Cauvin, a young attorney-turned-standup, who called Greg "the patron saint to every new comedian." At his audition, Cauvin performed a bit that he had previously done on *The Late Late Show*, and that he admitted was a little generic and hacky. The writing was clever, but the basis of the joke — comparing one parent's ethnicity to the other's — seemed overused. Greg appreciated the joke's execution but critiqued its concept. "I've already heard 20 different people come in with 'my father is this, my mother is that,'" said Greg. Cauvin understood and appreciated Greg's comments. "It was a very gentle letdown from my idol," said Cauvin.

Tom Clark, a well-respected and easygoing comedian from Wisconsin, worked his way through the Los Angeles comedy scene in the early 2000s. Clark had tried out for *Last Comic Standing* in previous seasons and had a poor experience each time. But his attitude changed with Greg in the mix.

"I worked with Andy Kindler and Natasha Leggero before," Clark said. "But I had never worked with Greg, so I wasn't sure what to expect."

Not known for being a particularly dark or edgy comedian, Clark decided to play off his Midwestern charm during his audition. "Hey, guys, I'm going to hit on a lot of hot-button issues, so you might want to buckle up," he said at the start of his set.

Hoping that the judges would pick up on his sarcasm, he continued with a bit about same-sex couples.

"I like gay people because they get to call each other partner — like they're detectives." The joke went over decently well with the audience, but Greg sat stone-faced at the judges' table.

Clark then transitioned to one of his more popular jokes.

"Growing up, my parents were very homopho-bic," said Clark. He quickly corrected the "mistake" and said, "Sorry, they were very *homm*-o-phobic — they hated words that sounded the same but meant something completely different." Clark tagged the joke with: "God made Adam and Eve not Adam and Atom."

Greg cracked a smile. Leggero and Kindler gave positive feedback. Clark waited nervously, anticipating Greg's reaction. "Yeah, that was pretty funny," said Greg.

Clark was ecstatic to get Greg's approval because he felt he was Greg's style of comic.

"So even him saying I was 'pretty funny' meant a lot," said Clark.

Greg also dealt constructive criticism. One contestant discussed a drug overdose. Greg rarely got angry while judging, but the matter-of-fact nature of this joke hit a nerve with him. He was furious and shared his irritation with Kindler.

"What he was basically saying is, 'Look, you asshole, I'm actually in pain,'" said Kindler of Greg's reaction. "'And you're treating it like a funny bit.' I was actually surprised how angry he was."

Greg introduced Kindler to new comedians. One comic was Mike DeStefano, who grew up in the Bronx and spoke about his battles with addiction. He was not an ironic, alternative comic. With his short gray hair and tattooed forearms, DeStefano looked more like a steelworker than a Hollywood performer. Greg was a fan. "This guy's really funny," he said to Kindler, who had never heard of him.

Midway through his televised set, DeStefano said, "I met a girl recently. And I was talking to her and said, 'Let's go have dinner.'"

"She said, 'I'm bulimic.' I said, 'How come you don't have an accent?'"

The crowd laughed. DeStefano continued, "She said, 'It's a disease.'"

"I said, 'I'll get some condoms. Don't worry about it.'"

After an applause break, DeStefano awaited the judges' reaction.

Kindler praised his consistency. "You made me laugh in the beginning and end," Kindler said. "In the middle, I'm laughing. And afterwards, I'm thinking about it and still laughing." Leggero also loved his act.

Greg lifted both his arms, smiled proudly, and said, "Great material. Great point of view — consistent point of view . . . you were funny from the minute you got out there. Awesome."

DeStefano became a show favorite and finished fourth that season.

Last Comic Standing allowed some comedians to appear outside of the open-call format. Patti Vasquez, Greg's friend from Chicago, was one of them. Although reluctant to fly to Los Angeles, Vasquez made it on time and was ready to perform. She had no idea Greg was a judge. Her act dealt with motherhood, and it garnered little appeal from Kindler and Leggero. Greg, on the other hand, adored it. After her set, he said, "You know I love you."

Greg's kind words weren't enough for her to advance. After the audition, Greg rushed backstage to reconnect with Vasquez. Greg told her that they had already seen several comics who discussed motherhood. He suggested that being viewed as a "mom comic" might have hurt her chances of moving forward.

It had been several years since Vasquez had seen Greg in person. He looked thinner than she remembered and seemed exhausted. She thought Greg's weariness might have resulted from watching so many comedians. But she also wondered if there was more to it. She asked Greg if he was okay. He shrugged off her question and gave her one final hug.

"As much as I was not thrilled about going to L.A. for *Last Comic Standing*," said Vasquez, "it gave me the gift of seeing him one more time."

Last Comic Standing heightened Greg's profile. He enjoyed mentoring comics and bantering with the judges. But there were aspects of the job that he disliked. Dylan Gadino said that "off the record, Greg said it was a good gig, but it was kind of monotonous." There was a lot of waiting around on the set, and though Greg was happy for the money, he wasn't passionate about the show.

Greg appeared as a guest on other TV shows as well. He was a regular on Lewis Black's *Root of All Evil*, which aired for 18 episodes in 2008. The format involved pitting two comedians against one another to debate a topic. One would make a case for whether one evil was greater than another. Winners were declared based on an audience poll and Black's decision. Greg appeared on the first episode and ultimately lost. But he did win the audience poll in advocating for the Catholic Church over Oprah (argued by Paul F. Tompkins). In the show's second-to-last episode, Greg lost again but persuaded the audience in advocating for strip clubs over sororities (argued by Kathleen Madigan).

Greg did a pilot for a trivia show called *Can You Stump Greg Giraldo?*, hosted by Greg Fitzsimmons. The idea was to test contestants' knowledge against Greg's. It borrowed from the format of *Win Ben Stein's Money,* a Comedy Central game show that ran from 1997 to 2003. The show suited Greg's wide-ranging knowledge and native intelligence. "He just knew everything about every topic," said a person who attended the pilot taping. "Of course, he didn't know everything off the top of his head, but he'd figure out the answer very quickly and his thinking process was always amazing."

Fitzsimmons, on the other hand, felt that Greg's work fell short of his usual standards: "Towards the end I don't think he was doing . . . a lot of great stuff. We did two pilots together in the year and a half before he died and he was not as focused as I had seen in the past. He was just not bringing himself to the project as much as I was used to seeing."

In 2010, Greg provided a hilariously memorable performance as a guest panelist on *The Marriage Ref,* a series hosted by Tom Papa and produced by Jerry Seinfeld. In each episode, celebrity guests would sound off on contentious issues submitted by married couples. They would then advise Papa on what person was right and what decision should be made.

In the episode that aired on May 6, 2010, Greg, Gwyneth Paltrow, and Seinfeld all joked about Greg's failing marriage. Greg mentioned that he had spent half the day with his divorce lawyer. In reality, he and MaryAnn were in mediation proceedings but never finalized their divorce. This show featured arguably the world's most famous comedian, an A-list, Oscar-winning actress, and one of his closest friends. And Greg was supposed to stick out. No easy task. Greg handled it with aplomb. "He was poised, he was funny," said Papa. "He stole the show."

Four couples addressed topics impacting their marriages. One husband was upset with his wife's refusal to reply quickly to his cell phone calls. Another man grew frustrated with his spouse for not dressing "hot" enough by South Beach standards. A knife-throwing husband resented his wife's reluctance to be his next subject. A wife's excessive snoring caused her husband to leave the bedroom in favor of sleeping with their dogs.

There was a friendly rapport among the three guests and the host. They all laughed and joked with one another. Greg addressed the cell phone husband, who had asked who was Brad Pitt's girlfriend in 1999. The camera panned to Paltrow, who faux-defensively said, "It wasn't me, it wasn't me," and then moved her arms in a victory gesture and ended with, "*Nineteen ninety-four*, baby!" Greg laughed along with the audience.

Greg commented that the cell phone husband was "taking the very unusual step of stalking his wife while they're still happily married."

Greg was relaxed. He delivered jokes calmly and allowed others to interject. He assumed a put-on angry attitude for the show. On a standup stage, Greg's comedy could be harsh—especially on the topic of marital discord—but here, he treated it all like a lark. He playfully dug into the other judges: "Everyone's so happy. You know, he's so happy. You're so happy, Gwyneth—look at her, with the rock star. They're happy. All we do is look into each other's eyes, and we burn piles of money."

After Greg's rant, Seinfeld said: "We gotta get more people on the show in the middle of ugly divorces."

While discussing the South Beach couple, the panel had fun with the husband for demanding that his wife wear "stripper chic" outfits. Greg and Seinfeld played off the husband's hard-line view on his wife's fashion choices. Greg made a crack about the woman's "secretly closeted husband" and Seinfeld added "not that there's anything wrong with that," referencing the famous line from his sitcom. The ribbing went back and forth as the panel bantered about who might or might not be gay. At the end of the segment, Greg asked, fake seriously, whether the husband had been involved in "*musical* theater."

Some of Greg's edgier standup style seeped out briefly while discussing the knife-throwing husband. He said, "Having spent the day talking to my divorce lawyer, I'm all for women getting knives thrown at them." But that was an anomaly. Throughout the episode, Greg was comfortable, engaged, and hilarious.

The *Marriage Ref* episode is a little-known gem of Greg's career. Readily available online, it shows him at a professional apex, if only for the 42 minutes of a network show. He's not the sweaty beginner. He's not the stinging roaster. He's not the road-weary headliner. He's centered, funny, and generous as if the best of Greg Giraldo shone for a while in a perfect little venue.

Chapter 12
Final Days

The way he went out was the least interesting thing about his life . . . The interesting thing about Greg Giraldo was his art.

— Ron Bennington

During the producers' after party for the Larry the Cable Guy roast on March 1, 2009, in Los Angeles, Greg met Michelle Paul, an attorney whom he thought looked like Angelina Jolie. Greg—sober at the time—made an instant connection with her. They discussed their legal backgrounds and quickly bonded. Greg and Michelle went on their first date in New York City later that month.

In June 2009, Greg moved out of Joe Schrank's apartment and rented his own one-bedroom apartment on the Upper West Side. His bedroom was crammed with a full-sized bed for himself, along with a twin-sized bed and bunk beds to accommodate his three sons when they visited.

Money was in short supply when he released his first and only one-hour special on Comedy Central titled *Midlife Vices*. Greg picked the title based on the name of a cover band in San Francisco. He couldn't afford to fund the entire project by himself, so he reached out to others for assistance.

On *Midlife Vices*, Greg again teamed up with Joel Gallen, who served as director and producer. "We did it really down and dirty over two nights," said Gallen, who led the production at the Union Square Theatre in New York City. They filmed the show on June 17 and 18, 2009—splicing the best pieces from each evening. "At some point, I realized he couldn't afford to actually pay me," Gallen said. "And, more importantly, he couldn't afford to pay the lighting guy and some of the other people that I sort of convinced to do it for next to nothing because I wanted the show to look good." Concerned that the crew wouldn't get paid, Gallen contacted Greg's agent and others who ultimately helped contribute more funding. "Eventually, money trickled in," Gallen said. "Some of those people did get paid or got paid half."

Greg's *Midlife Vices* special aired on August 16, 2009. Reviews were generally quite favorable. *Punchline Magazine* named it the number one comedy album of 2009. Sean L. McCarthy called it "great stuff" and noted Greg's "knack for blending serious political commentary with outrageous social material and finding the hard-hitting joke."

Here are some excerpts from the special:

> *You see these little fat kids in parks. They don't even walk. They just come gliding by on those Heely wheels. Fat kids on wheels: is that a good idea, do you think? Kids don't burn any calories in the modern world — now we put wheels on them? What the fuck? Why don't we just bolt the*

wheels directly into their spines? This way, they don't even have to sit up. They can lay flat on their back and we can roll them around from snack to snack.

There are more whipped men on television than there were on the Amistad.

Sports are way too important to people in America. Holy shit. It's like the new opiate of the masses; it just keeps people from realizing how fucked they actually are, you know. Let's face it: if you couldn't get drunk and paint yourself orange and brown every Sunday, you might realize, "Shit. I live in Cleveland. How the fuck did this happen? How did I end up in this frozen shithole?"

About seven months after wrapping *Midlife Vices,* Greg received a surprise request from the show's producer. Joel Gallen had a high school reunion coming up on October 1, 2010, on Long Island. His classmates had asked him to book entertainment for the event. Gallen had not received any payment for his work on *Midlife Vices,* so he decided to barter with Greg. "Do my reunion," Gallen said to Greg over the phone. He added, "Listen, I don't mean to guilt you, but last I checked, you still owe me some money." Gallen would forgive the debt if Greg performed standup for his high school friends. Happy to hear from his old buddy, Greg said, "Of course I'll do that." This 15-minute set would give

Greg a chance to make amends and help Gallen look good at his class reunion. Greg contacted his agent to set up a weekend of shows in early October at a club in Levittown—a 10-minute drive from Gallen's reunion site.

Greg emailed Gallen to confirm his availability. "I did in fact book the club in Levittown. I'm going to tear the island up!" wrote Greg. "I feel less guilty now since you will sort of be paid."

Gallen would arrange for a car to pick up Greg between shows at the club and take him to the Long Island Marriott in Uniondale, New York, for the reunion. Initially, Gallen intended to keep Greg's performance a secret. He couldn't do it. He leaked the news. Rumors of Greg's private performance spread quickly.

In March 2010, Dylan Gadino interviewed Greg for *Punchline Magazine*, describing him as looking "refreshed and happy." But Gadino wasn't sure whether Greg was using drugs or not: "During that interview, he seemed great. He was thin, but not super thin . . . He was jittery. Before the interview started, he ran across the street to some bodega and got some sort of trail mix or some shit like that. He was like, 'Yeah, if I don't eat, my ADD will be crazy' . . . He seemed a little hyper . . . He was in good spirits, though. He seemed like he was in a really good place."

Jim Norton co-hosted the Nasty Show with Greg at the Montreal Comedy Festival that summer. He had some concerns. "I wondered if he was drinking," said Norton. "He was spending most of his time in his dressing room and not kind of hanging and interacting . . . A lot of times I kind of knew when he was using again because I'd be like, 'Hey man, how are you?' And he's like, 'Ah, you know, a little rough,' or he'd go, 'Oh, I'm doing really good.' I would just kind of ask him a basic question and we both knew what I was asking."

By the summer of 2010, Greg began to search for a larger apartment that could more comfortably accommodate his three sons. He kept in regular contact with MaryAnn, who helped arrange visits with their boys. Although he did his best to be on time for his meetings, his addiction hindered his punctuality, and even caused him to fail to show up to some meetings at all. Greg nonetheless maintained a loving relationship with his children while he tried to improve his condition. His situation did improve for a while. He ate healthier. He exercised regularly. He worked to get better. But his efforts were hampered by self-doubt and addiction.

In the middle of September 2010, Greg scheduled a doctor's appointment. He sought advice to help set him on a healthier path. The appointment did not go well. On his way out of the doctor's office, Greg ran into comedian Louis Ramey, who was on his way to an audition near Times Square. Greg had known Ramey since the late 1990s when they both worked the club circuit in New York City and on

Long Island. Ramey would occasionally give Greg a lift to Rascals when Greg didn't want to drive his motorcycle.

Circumstances were far less upbeat during this reconnection. Greg said to Ramey that his doctor had told him to stop drinking and doing drugs. But Greg felt little hope of success. "I'm just going to die," he said. "I don't think I can do this. I don't think I can quit drinking."

Ramey was baffled by what Greg was saying. From his point of view, Greg's professional life was going great. It appeared that breakthrough success was right around the corner for him. Ramey said, "You need to just reassess things, because it might be hard, but it's worth it. It's worth the battle."

But Ramey noticed that his attempts to comfort Greg were not working. "There wasn't anything I could do at that point," said Ramey, who continued on to his audition.

Later that month, Greg performed at the Stress Factory in New Brunswick, New Jersey, in what turned out to be his final shows. Comedian Melvin George II opened for him. George, who had performed with Greg in the 1990s, marveled at Greg's knack for winning over audiences.

"His honesty knew no depths," George said about Greg's stage work.

On Thursday, September 23, 2010, Greg kicked off the first of a planned four-day slate of shows.

From backstage, George admired Greg's fluidity. He couldn't tell what material was improvised and what was rehearsed. Greg bounced topics off audience members and took them on his classic tangents. He did pop-culture material but he also addressed some personal struggles, such as a pending divorce and dating in your 40s.

That night, after his second show, Greg was supposed to meet Michelle in Virginia. Instead, he partied in New Brunswick. He had done similar things before, and this time Michelle got so upset that she considered ending the relationship. The next day Greg texted Michelle and apologized profusely. He said he would stop drinking if she came to his shows that night.

Michelle was already on her way to New York City to visit a friend, but she turned around and drove back to New Jersey. She arrived at the Stress Factory Friday evening in time to catch part of Greg's second show.

On Saturday, Greg was scheduled to appear at the third annual New York Recovery Rally, an event that Joe Schrank helped promote as part of National Alcohol and Drug Addiction Recovery Month. Greg never made it to the gathering. He texted Schrank before the rally to say: "I can't do it, I'm sorry."

Another group of excited comedy fans filled the Stress Factory on Saturday night. George warmed up the crowd as he had on Thursday and Friday. But when it was time to finish his set, he didn't see the red light. He noticed something else. The club owner, Vinnie Brand, was moving his hands in and out frantically, indicating that George had to stretch out his set. Minutes later, Brand walked on the stage and announced that Greg had been taken to the hospital.

Greg did not perform at the Stress Factory that night. Nor did he make it to Gallen's reunion.

Greg's Last Standup Performances

Giraldo fan Andrew Suydam attended the first of the two shows on September 24, 2010. This is his account of the performance.

A few things that I noticed with seeing Greg perform live that night: he seemed a bit off compared to when he was on television. If you remember Greg from the Comedy Central roasts and standup specials, you would notice that bright energy that he had on television. This particular night, that energy didn't seem to be there . . . During his set, he even apologized to the audience if he appeared upset because he and his wife were going through a divorce . . .

He was still very funny and entertaining to watch. The audience laughed at all his jokes, so in a way, the show itself was "successful." Some of the jokes that he did that night were repeats from his specials, like "Did you hear about the horse with the fucked-up leg? Paul McCartney's ex-wife!" Or how difficult it would be for Tiger Woods to "just explain" to his wife that he wanted to bang other girls. There was also one where he said that calling strip clubs "gentlemen's clubs" was falsely titled . . . However, despite the repeated jokes, there were some that I felt were new. Greg commented on Katy Perry wearing a low-cut shirt on *Sesame Street*. Although I don't remember word for word what the Katy Perry joke was, I remember the punch line was basically him saying that "kids are too distracted by puppet monsters to notice boobs," or something like that.

After the show, Greg did a meet-and-greet. I bought a copy of his DVD standup special called *Midlife Vices*. He signed it with a message that reads: "Andrew, Stay real!—Greg Giraldo." Overall, during my encounter with Greg, he was as nice as anyone could be despite his announced depression. He took photos with everyone, signed anything you could have given to him, etc.

Friday night had not gone well.

By the time Michelle arrived at the Stress Factory, a fan had already given Greg some of her own prescription pain medication and Roxicet (oxycodone) and sold him cocaine. Greg took the pills, snorted the coke, and continued drinking.

After the second show on Friday, Greg met with fans and signed autographs. He and Michelle didn't make it to their room at the Hyatt till about 2 a.m. She tried to go to sleep, as she had been up since Thursday worrying about Greg. However, his persistent attempts to talk to her prevented it. She grew so tired that she said she needed to leave to visit her friend in New York.

Greg begged her to stay. She did for a while. A few hours later though, Greg left the room without saying where he was going. When he returned, Michelle was gone. She had packed her bags and driven to New York to get some rest.

After she left, Greg sent her a few texts, including a final one: "I am sorry. This is not your fault."

Michelle arrived safely at her friend's place and slept there through the day. Meanwhile, Greg had called the fan with the Roxicet and asked for more. She was in his room around 12:30 on Saturday afternoon. Alcohol bottles covered the coffee table. Greg was incredibly upset. He told her that Michelle had left him due to his drinking. She listened to him for a while and then he fell asleep. She left once Greg started snoring, assuming he would be fine.

Around 5 p.m. on Saturday, Michelle called Greg. He didn't answer, so she drove straight to New York, fearing something had happened to him. She arrived at the hotel and ran to Greg's room as quickly as she could. She banged on the door repeatedly. There was no answer. However, she could hear the sound of his alarm going off. He had likely set it to wake himself up for the show.

"I knew that something terrible was happening because he never slept through that alarm," she said.

Michelle ran to the lobby and told the front desk employees that Greg might have overdosed. She and a hotel staff member rushed back to the room. They opened the door to find Greg lying on the bed shirtless wearing jeans, a belt, and necklaces. He didn't appear to be breathing. Michelle threw some water on his face and administered CPR. Around 8:20 p.m., a hotel employee called 911. An ambulance soon arrived, and paramedics revived Greg's pulse before taking him to Robert Wood Johnson University Hospital. There he remained in a coma assisted by a life-support machine.

Many relatives and friends visited Greg in the hospital. They included MaryAnn, Greg's mother, his siblings, and Michelle. On Tuesday, September 28, MaryAnn took Rick Dorfman to the hospital to see Greg. Dorfman cried as he held Greg's hand.

Greg died the next day after being removed from life support.

The reactions to Greg's passing were swift and heartfelt. The earliest tweets to mention his death started to post around 3 p.m. Louis CK was one of the first. Jim Norton confirmed the fact about two hours later. He announced that Greg had died and shared the last photo they took together, a picture of them at Noam Dworman's wedding.

Thousands of tweets rolled in lionizing Greg and his work. They came from comedians, friends, and fans. Lisa Lampanelli shared: "There are no words 2 express what a shame it is 2 lose Greg Giraldo. His smart humor was unparalleled & he will be missed for yrs to come."

Sarah Silverman tweeted: "RIP Greg Giraldo. Belly-laugh hilarious, prolific, good & kind. A thousand oys can't express."

Greg Fitzsimmons called Greg a great comedian and a great friend.

Actor and comedian Erik Passoja said that Greg was "an inspiration to all us up-and-coming comics back in the '90s." Standups who had auditioned for *Last Comic Standing* during Greg's tenure as a judge paid their respects as well. Chad Riden thanked him for "laughing at my stupid jokes & for telling me not to kill myself. You made my LCS audition actually fun." Elvis Collins remembered that Greg was one of the few judges to actually hang out with the comedians even when it wasn't being televised: "Greg Giraldo was the only one from Last Comic 7 who came out and talked to us on line without a camera following him. A class act."

Some called him "brave, brilliant and inspiring," saying he "had stuff that made comics strive to be better." Others celebrated Greg's kind acts. Pete Lee said that Greg "bought me groceries once on the road when I was at my poorest."

Jon Stewart used his platform on *The Daily Show* to pay homage to Greg. He changed the episode's "Moment of Zen" segment to the "Moment of Greg." Stewart said that he enjoyed running into Greg at comedy clubs because he was a "font of warmth and good humor and smart-as-hell comedy." The show concluded with a clip of Greg performing standup and a closing frame reading: "We'll miss you, brother."

Jon Stewart, Sarah Silverman, Chris Rock, and several other comedians joined Greg's family and friends to pay their respects during a two-night memorial at the Andrett Funeral Home in New York. Jessica Kirson and Judy Gold said it was a ceremony of sadness and mourning. Colin Quinn and Joe Schrank gave moving tributes. Comedian Ray Ellin said that Greg would have felt honored by the outpouring of love and support.

Amid their grief and emotion, family and friends offered comfort while appreciating Greg. John Giraldo shared a moving eulogy for his beloved brother, recalling stories from their childhood. Memories of joyful times were celebrated. Photographs were displayed throughout the venue, not just of Greg alone but also pictures of him with his three sons, playing, laughing, and sharing their love.

And there were reminders of the impression Greg had left in other parts of his life. The president of Regis High School couldn't say enough nice things about Greg, calling him a helpful, brilliant student.

Greg's family also organized a more intimate burial ceremony in the Hamptons. Limited to family members and close friends, the funeral followed Catholic traditions. There were customary rites, processions, and readings. Mourners shared their love and prayers as Greg was laid to rest. Inscribed on his tombstone was the epitaph:

Beloved Father

Always Loved

Forever Remembered

A sign reading "Gone Boating" decorated his grave.

Upon hearing the news of Greg's passing, Jamie Masada broke down and wondered if there was anything he could do. That evening Masada placed a message on the Laugh Factory marquee that read: "Greg Giraldo. Rest in Peace. Make God Laugh."

Masada walked on stage to deliver an impromptu announcement. "We lost one of our greats, a member of our family . . . He loved to make people laugh," he said. "We want everybody that knew him, and those that didn't know him—we want you to stand up." The crowd took to its feet. Masada conducted the packed house to offer beautiful sounds of laughter and applause to Greg. "Send him to God," Masada directed from the stage. "Send him to God."

Everyone stood up for nearly 15 minutes. They applauded, laughed, and wiped tears from their faces.

"That's how we sent him to God," said Masada.

Chapter 13

How He's Remembered

*I don't think he would want to be known as anything
other than a great comedian.*

        – Patrick Melton

On November 2, 2010, several comedians gathered
at the Comix comedy club in New York City's
Meatpacking District to roast Jim Florentine, a comic
known for his love of heavy metal music and for his
Special Ed character on *Crank Yankers*. The set
included an empty seat on the stage in
remembrance of Greg, who had been scheduled to
perform. Proceeds from the event went to support
the Greg Giraldo Children's Fund. In a fitting
gesture, Jesse Joyce replaced Greg in the lineup.
During Joyce's introduction, host Rich Vos said, "If
you Google his name, it'll come back, 'Why?'" Joyce,
a relative unknown to many in attendance, showed
no signs of nervousness and offered his own eulogy
for Greg.

"It's kind of bittersweet for me to be here," said
Joyce. "This was going to be the next project we
worked on together . . . A couple weeks before he
died, he actually invited me to do this." Joyce continued: "I said, 'All right, what do you want to do
for it?' He told me, 'Ideally I would love to take an
entire bag of pharmaceuticals and stop my heart, so

I don't have to roast the Sebastian Bach of retard jokes.'"

After the applause break, Joyce said: "It was really tragic when Greg passed away. I think we all thought, *Why? Why couldn't it have been Vos?* The answer is because you can't overdose on ExtenZe and Crest White Strips."

The event progressed in a manner similar to most roasts. However, a palpable sense of loss remained throughout the show. Comedians mourned and honored Greg—while still entertaining the crowd. "These were Greg's friends doing what they've dedicated their lives to—making people laugh," wrote Dylan Gadino, who attended the roast. "But it was also his friends healing. And it was something special to see that happen."

Greg's life and character were full of conflict and contradictions: harsh and gentle, funny and insecure, blue collar and Ivy League. These facets also shape how he's remembered. The *New York Times* called Greg an "insult-humor comic" and *Entertainment Weekly* offered a terser description, referring to him as an "insult comedian." Even the *Harvard Crimson* reduced him to "insult comic." In part, such descriptions are a tribute to Greg's roast performances. In some ways though, they slight Greg's broader contributions.

MaryAnn Giraldo and her family remembered the happy times they had shared with Greg and celebrated his successes.

Those who knew Greg personally and professionally focused on his comedic brilliance and intriguing character. Nick Di Paolo initially joked that Greg would be remembered as "a weak feature act from Minnesota," but he then added: "I want them to think of him as the guy he was. He was smart, funny, had a dark side to him. You can tell there's still a lot of admiration for him. I don't know anybody that didn't like him. I really don't . . . Even in his passing, he's admired and rightfully so."

Gadino called Greg a "great comic" and said, "Part of me is just super sad that more generations of people won't be able to experience him live, because he really was a great performer."

J-L Cauvin lamented the loss of Greg and Patrice O'Neal, who died in 2011 at the age of 41 from complications from a stroke. Cauvin noted their impact as politically incorrect social commentators, not just comedians "who like to say *cunt* a lot." He characterized Greg and O'Neal as "strong voices who could have been really big voices."

Many knew Greg as a loyal friend and a warm person. Jessica Kirson called him a "very loving, kind soul" with "real love": "He was so accessible. A lot of male comics, you'll talk to them and as a woman or female comic they won't look you in the eye when they talk to you. He was like, 'Hey!' He would always give me a huge hug, he would kiss me, he'd sit with his arm around me. He was that kind of a person."

Megyn Price knew Greg as a caring friend. After their sitcom, *Common Law,* wrapped up, Greg stopped at her house on the way to the airport to return to New York. He was concerned for her health because the young actress had gotten so thin. She still remembered his words to her: "I just love you and you are so beautiful, and you would be so much more beautiful with another layer of you on you."

Michelle Paul called him "amazing, kind, warm, quite charismatic." She remembered small kindnesses that he did routinely, such as never reclining his seat on an airplane out of consideration for the space of the passenger behind him. He had what she called a "childlike quality" to him: "One time we were packing our stuff to leave a Dallas hotel room. We were listening to Bad Company—he'd go through phases where we'd listen to the same band or song over and over—and we were hurrying to pack up to catch our plane, and at some point we both found ourselves singing into a hairbrush. I stopped and said, 'We are not adults, Greg.' He laughed in agreement."

Natasha Leggero recalled the last text she had from Greg: "He was going in for a fitting with a costume designer that we had worked [with] before and he wanted to make sure he knew her name, so he texted me and was like, 'I don't want to not know this woman's name since I worked with her before.'"

Dom Irrera recounted fond memories of his fun-loving and teasable friend. They differed over soccer, with Greg defending the game as exciting and Irrera calling it a bore. "How could it be exciting with a zero-zero score?"

"It's not zero-zero; it's nil-nil," Greg said defensively, and Irrera mock-argued and fake-fought and replied sarcastically, "Well, *now* I see. Fun, fabulous fun now!" And that was the last time they talked.

Steven Siegel, Greg's colleague from his lawyer days, called him a sensitive person in both senses of the word: he was perceptive, but he was also vulnerable to criticism and harshness. "When Greg would be criticized by somebody, there was an element of vulnerability to it," Siegel said.

Jim Gaffigan remembered Greg's "inherent generosity," his being "the type of guy that you could call . . . at any moment," and said that he had "the characteristics you want in your children": "Loyal, compassionate, passionate, sympathetic, made of substance. He was never being friends with someone . . . because it would help his career."

Marc Maron didn't spend a lot of time with Greg, but "he understood me and he made me laugh. He always did. I would see him only sporadically and usually only for a few minutes to a half hour just sitting around. We never went to dinner. We never did drugs together. We never did anything together. I rode on the back of his motorcycle once, but every time I saw him, it was like seeing a best friend, and that's a rare quality."

The central theme in people's remarks on Greg's legacy, which virtually all his peers reiterated, was that he was simply one of the most talented and hardest-working comedians ever. It was an overwhelming consensus. Judy Gold said that he was simply one of the best: "His voice was silenced way too soon and it was tragic. I think he should be remembered for the incredible writer and performer that he was . . . He was a great guy and he had such a drive . . . He was a great thinker."

Colin Quinn said that Greg was "underrated," like Mitch Hedberg and Patrice O'Neal. Jim Norton said that Greg supplemented his natural skills with hard work: "I think they perceived him as a really smart and funny and prolific guy. I don't think people had a bad perception of him . . . As far as being a comedian, his reputation was excellent. Greg had a great reputation as a comic and as a guy who worked. So, no, I think that the way he's remembered is as a hilarious roaster and a guy who was just like, 'Fuck, man, we really miss seeing him rip people apart.'"

Price said Greg derived "pure joy" from making people laugh. "It was never about ego . . . It was not that he felt good about himself when he made people laugh. It's just he felt good about the universe when he made people laugh. He felt good about you when he made you laugh . . . His pure focus was to make other people happy."

Several comedians respected Greg's comedic integrity. Jay Mohr: "Greg Giraldo was a great, not good, *great* comedian. There is a question that comics always ask themselves, 'Why isn't *that* guy on television?' You don't know what being in somebody's head on a daily basis—you don't know how they handle interpersonal communication. You don't know their self-sabotaging ways. I don't know if Greg—what he did behind closed doors in rooms with executives. But Greg stayed true to comedy, what he wanted to do in comedy. He stayed exactly, he played that set list perfectly. And he would not waver."

Greg Fitzsimmons said that Greg "wouldn't look at it as a failure that he didn't get in TV or movies or whatever that was because I think his heart and passion was in standup, and I think he got everything out of that. I think he put a lot into it and I think he got everything out of it that he put into it." Greg also served as an inspiration and a mentor to younger comedians. As Ted Alexandro noted: "He actually gave encouragement verbally, but . . . just seeing him and knowing he was there was encouragement for me because . . . he was dealing in a style that in some way I aspired to . . . I just remember him as a fierce and significant talent who was awe-inspiring."

Finally, Joel Gallen put Greg's success in context: "I think Greg should be remembered as one of the great comics of all time, and I mean that whole-heartedly. He stands toe to toe with all the great ones. He had his voice, which was very special and very unique, and incredibly hilarious. I hold him in the highest regard as anybody would hold a Jerry Seinfeld or a George Carlin or a Dave Chappelle or a Chris Rock. I think he's definitely an unsung hero and probably will never get the recognition he deserved, but for me, he stands alone, near the top of the mountain."

Despite the many disappointments, Greg made it up that mountain. He took a great risk in leaving a legal career to pursue a life in comedy, but he did so without regret. And he made it.

Onstage, Greg was brave, vulnerable, and honest. Offstage, he was a willing mentor and approachable friend. He loved his three sons beyond measure. He was admired for his warm compassion and his intelligence. But he is remembered most of all for his brilliant comedy.

"Little did I know that earning a living at stand-up is the hardest thing you can do," Greg said. "But once I started doing it, I just loved it, and I realized that I was actually kinda good at it, and then that was it."

Notes

"Interview" refers to an original interview by the authors of the people listed in the Sources on pages 279–280. "Interview with a source" indicates an interview with a reliable person whom the authors are choosing to keep anonymous. "Ibid." indicates the same source as in the previous note.

Chapter 1. The Smart Kid

p1 **"Somebody as smart"** Interview with Alexandro.
p1 **"All that and much more"** Interview with a source.
p4 **"It was a cool time"** Interview with Livio.
p4 **"Once inside"** Kurson, "Who's killing the great lawyers of Harvard?"
p5 **"He was such a good boy"** Interview with Whitaker.
p5 **"Early one evening"** Ibid.
p6 **"Greg took an interest in Robin Lazarus"** Interview with Whitaker.
p8 **"We were big drinkers"** Interview with Miller.
p8 **"Total shithole"** Ibid.
p10 **"He volunteered several hours each week"** Interview with Glaser.
p11 **"Columbia's Ivy League rigor"** Kurson, "Who's killing the great lawyers of Harvard?" ; Interview with Kurson.
p11 **"I probably should"** Interview with Glaser.
p12 **"Dragged along by fate"** Dixit, "Greg Giraldo on failure."
p12 **"To enter Harvard Law School"** Interview with Ellin ; Interview with Weiner.
p12 **"Dave Diamond, a friendly and witty first-year student"** Interview with Diamond.
p13 **"Greg had to find an outfit"** Kurson, "Who's killing the great lawyers of Harvard?" ; Interview with Kurson.

Chapter 2. Lawyer and Comedian

Chapter 3. Common Law: The Sitcom

p42 **"Greg's performance at the New Faces show"** Ibid.

p46 **"I have this great idea"** Interview with Price.

p46 **"Oh, it's an honor"** Ibid.

p48 **"Maria, why would"** "Pilot," *Common Law*, season 1, episode 1, ABC, Sept. 28, 1996.

p48 **"I'm not a particularly emotional man"** Ibid.

p52 **"Greg and Ray"** Interview with Joyce.

p52 **"Ah, this is my big shot"** Ibid.

p53 **"ABC aired only four"** Brooks and Marsh, *The complete directory to prime time network and cable TV shows, 1946–present.*

p53 **"Hugely upsetting"** Interview with LaZebnik.

p53 **"Series of events"** P., "An Interview with Greg Giraldo."

p54 **"We both sort of knew"** Interview with Klein.

p55 **"Jamie Tarses"** P., "An Interview with Greg Giraldo."

p55 **"Spanish it up"** Ibid.

p55 **"I hadn't really been exposed"** Ibid.

p56 **"A million examples"** Ibid.

p56 **"Because I grew up"** Lipton, et al., "TV's most fascinating people."

p56 **"I'm the torchbearer"** Ibid.

p56 **"He never once denied"** Interview with Julian Barba.

p57 **"It undermines your accomplishment"** Weinstein, "Something uncommon about 'Law.'"

p57 **"He lost his agent"** Interview with Gaffigan. (*It's possible Greg worked with other agents within the same agency during the time period described.*)

Chapter 4. Marriage and Family

p59 **"Special thanks to"** G. Giraldo, *Good day to cross a river.*

p59 **"With 300 seats"** Miller, "Gotham's first lady of funny."

p60 **"We went from hanging out"** Interview with M. Giraldo.

p62 **"Look at this jerkoff"** Interview with Lievano.

p62 **"It's all good"** Ibid.

p63 **"Are you sure"** Ibid.

p63 **"Throughout the car ride"** Ibid.

p64 **"It was in a small bar"** Interview with Paroly.

p66 **"Are you calling me"** Interview with M. Giraldo.

p68 **"Wow, you've been really lucky"** Ibid.

p70 **"For that little brief moment"** Bennington, "Greg Giraldo: A life in comedy."

p72 **"I didn't tell you"** G. Giraldo, *Good day to cross a river*.

p72 **"Well, I hate"** Ibid.

p75 **"Greg, you're full of shit"** Interview with Schrank.

p75 **"You can't go"** Interview with M. Giraldo

p76 **"As Greg's drinking issues worsened"** Ibid.

p76 **"All I want"** Ibid.

p77 **"At that point"** Ibid.

Chapter 5. A Comedian's Mind

p79 **"I thought open mics"** Interview with Dixit.

p80 **"I'm constantly tortured"** Dixit, "Greg Giraldo on failure."

p80 **"I'm not a"** Ibid.

p80 **"I get all fucking ADD"** Ibid.

p81 **"It's confirmation bias"** Interview with Dixit.

p81 **"It's not so much the jokes"** Serota, "Greg Giraldo."

p81**"That was such an insane thing"** Interview with Quinn.

p82 **"An internal experience of intellectual phoniness that researchers say"** Sakulku and Alexander, "The impostor phenomenon."

p82 **"Strengthening the feeling of being a fraud or an impostor"** Sakulku and Alexander, "The impostor phenomenon."

p82 **"Some people do better"** Dixit, "Greg Giraldo on failure"

p82 **"Comedy is fucking hard!"** Interview with Dixit.

p83 **"I know people who have played"** Interview with Leggero.

p83 **"Stanhope was also a fan of Greg"** Stanhope, "Giraldo."

p84 **"Cook 'crushed'"** Interview with Gallen.

p85 **"Stayed true to comedy"** Interview with Mohr.

p86 **"Greg and Schrank made a series of online videos"** Interview with Schrank.

p86 **"Jessica Kirson referred to the comedian"** Interview with Kirson.

p87 **"More than 10 percent of the population"** Interview with Merrill.

p87 **"The overall result for Greg"** Interview with Schrank.

p88 **"His biggest fault"** Interview with Price.

p88 **"He wanted everyone around him to be happy"** Interview with Johnson.

p88 **"I'm living the life I've always wanted"** Ibid.

Chapter 6. Tough Crowd

p89 **"It was a bit menacing"** Czajkowski, "'It was a fighter's comedy show': The oral history of 'Tough Crowd with Colin Quinn.'"

p89 **"We need to talk"** Interview with Gaffigan.

p90 **"*We* have been the cowards"** *Politically Incorrect.*

p90 **"I have to leave"** The N.Y. Friars Club Roast of Hugh Hefner.

p90 **"We're going to be okay"** Interview with Alexandro.

p92 **"Greg could crush"** Interview with Shillue.

p93 **"This was like"** Interview with Norton.

p93 **"You gotta give Lorne Michaels credit"** Czajkowski, "'It was a fighter's comedy show': The oral history of 'Tough Crowd with Colin Quinn.'"

p94 **"That's what really created"** Interview with Maron.

p95 **"There was no agenda"** Interview with Sairs.

p96 **"*Tough Crowd* looks especially"** James, "Television: They're celebrities, and you're not."

p96 **"Which deserves all the extravagant praise"** Ibid.

p97 **"I can do this"** Interview with Czajkowski.

p97 **"Colin would walk in"** Interview with Norton.

p98 **"He never let the show down"** Interview with Quinn.

p98 **"Do you know how short"** *Tough Crowd with Colin Quinn.*

p99 **"Maybe there's a nonviolent way"** Ibid.

p99 **"There's a nonviolent way"** Ibid.

p99 **"I heard they'll agree"** Ibid.

p100 **"You're the guy"** Ibid.

p100 **"And if you had tried"** Ibid.

p100 **"One of the greatest"** Interview with Hofstetter.

p100 **"There's no better moment"** Czajkowski, "'It was a fighter's comedy show': The oral history of 'Tough Crowd with Colin Quinn.'"

p100 **"If you get drunk"** *Tough Crowd with Colin Quinn.*

p101 **"He didn't want people to think"** Interview with Shillue.

p101 **"I didn't wimp out"** Ibid.

p101 **"It was a great moment"** *Give it up for Greg Giraldo.*

p101 **"That was good TV"** Interview with Quinn.

p101 **"Some suggested"** Interview with Diamond.

p101 **"Patched it up"** Interview with Shillue.

p101 **"Something weird happened"** Interview with Klein.

p102 **"He was always going for the joke"** Interview with Norton.

p102 **"Giraldo could swing"** Interview with Czajkowski.

p103 **"Giraldo could deliver"** Interview with Di Paolo.

p103 **"Giraldo let some doozies"** Ibid.

p104 **"A sampling of their exchanges"** *These quotations from episodes of* Tough Crowd *are all taken from grainy YouTube videos of the show which are readily available online.*

p105 **"Yes, for these dummies"** *Tough Crowd with Colin Quinn.*

p106 **"We should go out"** Ibid.

p106 **"The people that are in the media"** Ibid.

p106 **"I just had a moment"** Ibid.

p107 **"Was enraging to Colin"** Interview with Norton.

Chapter 7. Pilots, TV Appearances, Movies

p109 **"On a day-to-day"** Serota, "Greg Giraldo."

p109 **"That used to get to him"** Interview with Quinn.

p110 **"In the entertainment industry"** Interview with Gaffigan.

p110 **"He was a great comedian"** Ibid.

p111 **"They can't really be that dirty"** Interview with Diamond.

p111 **"Dude, I think"** Interview with Swardson.

p112 **"This felt like Greg's moment"** Ibid.

p112 **"It couldn't have gone better"** Ibid.

p112 **"Greg was devastated"** Ibid.

p112 **"Ah, fuck, man"** Ibid.

p112 **"Kelsey had a lot"** Ibid.

p113 **"People are in your ear"** Ibid.

p114 **"After the show"** Interview with Klein. (*Klein cited $800 as the amount paid. The actual amount may have been different.*)

p115 **"Greg allegedly didn't receive"** Ibid.

p115 **"I made tens"** Interview with Hofstetter.

p115 **"All he ever wanted"** Ibid.

p116 **"Don't be a loser"** OKCable, Television commercial.

p116 **"It's good for everyone"** Ibid.

p116 **"Merciless pop-culture commentary"** Fretts, "Meet the comic who gave Ray Romano a run for his money."

p116 **"I haven't even seen it yet"** Ibid.

p116 **"I'd watch that if my other choice"** Ibid.

p117 **"I got on the show"** *The Howard Stern Show*.

p117 **"He got paid for showing up"** Interview with Brill.

p118 **"Greg, it has nothing to do with you"** Interview with Brill.

p118 **"Greg didn't outright"** *The Late Show with David Letterman*, Mar. 4, 2005.

p119 **"He was just a little off"** Interview with Hogan.

p119 **"Untitled project, shot"** Martin, "New shot for old 'Crowd.'"

p120 **"You've got to do it"** Interview with Quinn.

p120 **"Greg was brilliant"** Czajkowski, "'It was a fighter's comedy show': The oral history of 'Tough Crowd with Colin Quinn.'"

p121 **"The various issues"** Milligan, "The Greg Giraldo Show pilot taping 4/7/05—Sony Studios."

p121 **"It can never be captured"** Ibid.

p122 **"Sent back to the shop"** Lafayette, "A showbiz companion."

p122 **"Ultimately, David Spade"** "Spade fronts Tinseltown send-up."

p122 **"Didn't want to fuck over"** Interview with Joyce.

p123 **"So here's the idea"** *Adult Content* pilot, on G. Giraldo, *Midlife Vices.*

p123 **"The one-hour pilot featured segments"** Byrnes, "Slick Argentinean staple looks to make trip to U.S."

p124 **"That pilot really captured his voice"** Interview with Klein.

p124 **"Not everybody gets a holding deal"** Interview with Diamond.

p124 **"I don't think he was ever"** Ibid.

Chapter 8. The Roasts

p127 **"Jeff Ross, I remember the exact moment"** *Comedy Central Roast of Donald Trump.*

p128 **"Though the partnership had been extremely lucrative"** DiGiacomo, "Jack Carter smothers brothers at rip-roaring friars roast."

p128 **"Jeff Ross sold the idea"** Interview with Kelly.

p128 **"It was just us celebrating"** Ibid.

p128 **"To me, it's what roasts"** Ibid.

p129 **"He was *not* an insult comic"** Interview with Dworman.

p129 **"So he got this opportunity"** Ibid.

p129 **"That was the least"** Ibid.

p129 **"He felt disappointed"** Interview with Alexandro.

p130 **"It's not a judgment of him"** Ibid.

p130 **"I guess that's the most easily disposable"** Ibid.

p130 **"Roast writing is such a specific, niche skill"** Interview with Joyce.

p131 **"He would call me and read"** Interview with Klein.

p131 **"This long production time created the angst"** Interview with Kindler.

p131 **"These are all unknowns"** The N.Y. Friars Club Roast of Chevy Chase.

p132 **"Oh, fuck you, I chopped off four"** Ibid.

p132 **"Chevy Chase was one of the first"** Serota, "Greg Giraldo."

p132 **"He was just angry"** Ibid.

p132 **"Nobody could have foreseen"** Interview with Kindler.

p133 **"His last one, though, was canceled"** "The Roast of Patrice O'Neal—Full."

p133 **"If you stay positive and work"** Ibid.

p133 **"How do you insult a guy"** Ibid.

p133 **"What kind of fucking ass-kissing shit"** Ibid.

p134 **"You gotta remember"** Ibid.

p134 **"She's agreed to do it"** Interview with Gallen.

p135 **"He walked into Herzog's office"** Ibid.

p135 **"We've got to have this guy"** Ibid.

p136 **"You're busier than Courtney Love's pharmacist"** *Comedy Central Roast of Pamela Anderson.*

p136 **"You starring in a show about books"** Ibid.

p137 **"I had to spend two nights"** Interview with Gallen.

p137 **"Which I'm thankful I was able to do"** Ibid.

p137 **"I basically kept my mouth shut"** Interview with Lievano.

p138 **"[Quotes from all comedians]"** *The Howard Stern Show,* "Roasting Gary Dell'Abate."

p139 **"You're trying not to bomb"** Interview with Fitzsimmons.

p139 **"You're very much aware"** Ibid.

p140 **"The comedians usually ended up with the edgier jokes"** Interview with Joyce.

p140 **"Norm's got a giant gambling problem"** *Comedy Central Roast of Bob Saget.*

p140 **"It's a fucking roast"** Ibid.

p140 **"You were an aide to Bobby Kennedy"** Ibid.

p140 **"That's a good fucking joke"** Ibid.

p140 **"Anyway, I'm sorry if the meanness"** Ibid.

p141 **"Katt, you're like Afro Sheen"** *Comedy Central Roast of Flavor Flav.*

p141 **"What a teeny little pimp"** Ibid.

p141 **"Disowned that roast after the fact"** Interview with Joyce.

p141 **"He seemed fine with it at the time"** Ibid.

p142 **"When you watch the roast"** Ibid.

p142 **"Like an idiot I tell him that"** Interview with Di Paolo.

p143 **"Dude, a lot of these are really great"** Interview with Joyce.

p144 **"Yeah, you're like the Vlasic pickle stork"** Ibid.

p144 **"Larry fucked his first cousin"** *Comedy Central Roast of Larry the Cable Guy*.

p144 **"How the *fuck* are you so *popular*?"** Ibid.

p144 **"It was just a genuine emotion"** Interview with Joyce.

p145 **"You make more money in a week"** *Comedy Central Roast of Larry the Cable Guy*.

p145 **"You gotta get over to his place"** Interview with Joyce.

p145 **"Then he checked Greg's pockets"** Ibid.

p146 **"Applying the finishing touches"** Ibid.

p146 **"When alcohol does its taxes"** *Comedy Central Roast of David Hasselhoff*.

p146 **"Your liver is so shriveled"** Ibid.

p148 **"It was just great to watch somebody"** Interview with Swardson.

p148 **"It was like a wrecking ball"** Ibid.

p148 **"I was like, 'No,'"** Ibid.

p149 **"Everybody ate it except for Greg"** Interview with Pompa.

p149 **"Greg said that Cheech was the only Mexican"** Ibid.

p149 **"A lot of people knew Greg from the roasts"** Interview with Quinn.

p151 **"And then your career dried up faster"** *Comedy Central Roast of Pamela Anderson*.

p152 **"If anything, it may have hurt his credibility"** Interview with Joyce.

p152 **"I thought the guy was a genius"** Interview with Kurson.

Chapter 9. Comedy and the Road

p171 **"Hey, you need work"** Interview with Joyce.

p171 **"We would be on the road"** Ibid.

p172 **"What do you got there?"** Ibid.

p172 **"He would take something of mine"** Ibid.

p173 **"Greg did grimy comedy club"** Interview with Schrank.

p174 **"I'm feeling so energized"** Interview with Paroly.

p174 **"I don't want to go home"** Ibid.

p174 **"First of all, it's certainly not sacred"** Giraldo, *Good day to cross a river.*

p175 **"I was on a plane the other day"** Ibid.

p176 **"I'm kidding, of course"** Ibid.

p176 **"Nobody has a dog"** Ibid.

p177 **"I'd been dreaming about this"** Interview with Melton.

p177 **"I can't do this bit"** Ibid.

p178 **"I just fucking melted"** Ibid.

p178 **"You're a funny person"** Ibid.

p178 **"I laughed my ass off"** Interview with Gadino.

p179 **"I was just blown away"** Interview with McCarthy.

p179 **"He had this way of being the smartest"** Ibid.

p179 **"He got from me a title of Doctor of the Soul"** Interview with Masada.

Chapter 10. Addiction

p182 **"Paroly received several messages"** Interview with Paroly.

p182 **"Wow, that's a different guy"** Ibid.

p183 **"I'm good now"** Opie and Anthony, XM Radio.

p183 **"It makes you much less funny"** Ibid.

p184 **"And then there was this Indian woman"** Ibid.

p184 **"She's pretending to sleep"** Ibid.

p184 **"Once the plane landed"** Ibid.

p185 **"Thanks for the 50 G's"** Ibid.

p185 **"I think that I'm done"** Ibid.

p185 **"People know what they have to do"** Ibid.

p186 **"If we can pray to God to help"** Ibid.

p186 **"I was so fucking busy"** Ibid.

p186 **"I'm not that comfortable in my skin"** Ibid.

p187 **"It's extremely common"** Interview with Merrill.

p187 **"I guess I was naïve"** Interview with Dworman.

p187 **"It was very apparent that he was suffering"** Interview with Adoram.

p188 **"Greg became irate with Jim Gaffigan"** Interview with Gaffigan.

p188 **"A few months later Mazzilli called"** Ibid.

p188 **"He would start drinking"** Interview with a source.

p188 **"Greg was the kind of guy"** Interview with Irrera.

p189 **"Why you got to get to the point"** Ibid.

p190 **"He just couldn't get it"** Interview with Kirson.

p190 **"He really had a hard time in AA"** Interview with Schrank.

p192 **"We both felt overwhelmed and insecure"** Schrank, "Greg Giraldo's last laugh."

p193 **"That's literally the only way"** Interview with Schrank.

p193 **"People who die of addiction"** Ibid.

p193 **"So we assume that's the case"** Interview with Merrill.

p193 **"And we do think of substance abuse"** Ibid.

p194 **"Okay, that's good, that's sober enough"** Winfrey, "Oprah recruits crackheads for Obama vote!"

p194 **"Oprah, how did you stop chewing"** Interview with Schrank.

p194 **"I remember when we did the"** Interview with Di Paolo.

p194 **"Nobody really enjoys this fucking comedy gig"** Interview with Kelly.

p195 **"I wouldn't want to walk around"** Interview with Mohr.

p196 **"It's my wife's name"** *Tattoo Fixation*.

p197 **"About a week later, Soto"** Interview with Masada.

p197 **"I look around. It's Richard"** Ibid.

p198 **"If things are going"** Interview with Tabori.

p198 **"You can see him starting"** Ibid.

p198 **"He was doing drugs *because*"** Ibid.

p198 **"And if they're not center stage"** Ibid.

p199 **"I'm actually fixing my problem"** Opie and Anthony.

p199 **"And then you try to stop"** Ibid.

p199 **"It gets fucking worse"** Ibid.

Chapter 11. Comic Standing

p202 *"Who the fuck am I"* Interview with Alexandro.

p203 **"I don't want to be an asshole"** Ibid.

p203 **"We're all just in the circus"** Ibid.

p203 **"I'm not going to sit"** Ibid.

p203 **"He had such a sweetness to him"** Interview with Kindler.

p203 **"Super intelligent, super funny, really sweet"** Interview with Leggero.

p204 **"We could laugh at each other"** Interview with Kindler.

p204 **"Greg seemed to always"** Interview with Leggero.

p204 **"I feel like having Greg Giraldo on"** Interview with Cauvin.

p204 **"I think he was one of the most respected"** Interview with Kaplan.

p205 **"She noticed that Greg"** Interview with Moore-sturgill.

p205 **"Hell, even 'from the cheap seats'"** Ibid.

p205 **"The patron saint"** Interview with Cauvin.

p205 **"I've already heard 20 different people"** Ibid.

Chapter 12. Final Days

p219 **"I wondered if he was drinking"** Interview with Norton.

p220 **"You need to just reassess"** Ibid.

p220 **"I'm just going to die"** Ibid.

p220 **"There wasn't anything"** Ibid.

p222 **"A few things that I noticed"** Interview with Suydam.

p223 **"But by the time Michelle arrived"** Interview with Paul.

p225 **"Michelle threw some water on his face and administered CPR. Around 8:20 p.m., a hotel employee called 911"** (*The details of what led up to that 911 call are unclear and different sources disagree on some key facts, primarily whether Greg was alone or with other people when he overdosed. One source insists that there was no party and Greg was alone in his room. However, Fox News reported initially that there was "a wild party in his room at the Hilton East Brunswick" (they had the hotel wrong). Anthony G. Attrino of NJ.com also reported, two years later, that there was a "wild party" in his room and that nobody called the police: "instead, the partiers left Giraldo alone in his room." The website Morbid New Jersey reported a year after he died that Greg "hung out with fans and drank at the Hyatt bar for a while" before the party moved to his room. "The party drifted into the early morning hours. No telling how many people were there, who they were or exactly what drugs they were using." For audio of the actual 911 call, see "Greg Giraldo 911 call – 'He's not breathing,'" TMZ.com.*)

p226 **"An inspiration to all"** Passoja, Twitter post.

p227 **"Bought me groceries"** Lee, Twitter post.

p228 **"The president of Regis High School"** Interview with Schrank.

p228 **"We lost one of our greats"** Interview with Masada.

Chapter 13. How He's Remembered

p231 **"If you Google his name"** Joyce, "Jesse Joyce @ The Cringe Humor Roast of Jim Florentine."

p232 **"These were Greg's friends"** Gadino, "Comedian friends joke about Greg Giraldo's death at roast."

p232 ***"The New York Times"*** O'Connor, "Greg Giraldo, insult-humor comic, dies at 44."

p232 ***"Entertainment Weekly"*** Ward, "Greg Giraldo: Remembering the great insult comedian."

p232 **"Even *The Harvard Crimson*"** Altman, "Greg Giraldo, comedian and former Harvard Law alumnus, dies."

p233 **"Nick Di Paolo initially joked"** Interview with Di Paolo.

p233 **"Gadino called Greg a 'great comic'"** Interview with Gadino.

p233 **"J-L Cauvin lamented the loss of Greg and Patrice O'Neal"** Interview with Cauvin.

p233 **"Jessica Kirson called him a 'very loving, kind soul'"** Interview with Kirson.

p234 **"Megyn Price knew Greg as a caring friend"** Interview with Price.

p234 **"Michelle Paul called him 'amazing, kind, warm, quite charismatic'"** Interview with Paul.

p234 **"Natasha Leggero recalled the last text"** Interview with Leggero.

p235 **"Dom Irrera recounted fond memories"** Interview with Irrera.

p235 **"Steven Siegel, Greg's colleague"** Interview with Siegel.

p235 **"Jim Gaffigan remembered Greg's 'inherent generosity'"** Interview with Gaffigan.

p235 **"Marc Maron didn't spend a lot of time with Greg"** Interview with Maron.

p236 **"Judy Gold said that he was simply one of the best"** Interview with Gold.

p236 **"Colin Quinn said that Greg was 'underrated'"** Interview with Quinn.

p236 **"Price said Greg derived"** Interview with Price.

p237 **"Jay Mohr"** Interview with Mohr.

p237 **"Greg Fitzsimmons"** Interview with Fitzsimmons.

p237 **"As Ted Alexandro noted"** Interview with Alexandro.

p238 **"Finally, Joel Gallen"** Interview with Gallen.

p238 **"The hardest thing you can do"** P., "An interview with Greg Giraldo."

Photographs

Four photographs of Greg and fellow students from Regis High School. Greg is in the white and dark plaid shirt. Art Miller is in the red plaid shirt. *(Art Miller)*

Greg at Regis.
(Robin Whitaker)

Greg (far right)
and friends.
(Robin Whitaker)

Greg with
Robin Lazarus,
his date, at his
high school
prom.
(Robin Whitaker)

Photographs

Greg (in the gray
three-piece suit)
at his high school
prom, held at the
Waldorf Astoria
hotel in NYC.
(Robin Whitaker)

263

Greg and his band playing at the
front steps of the library at Columbia
University. Greg is on the far left;
Mike Weiner is second from the right.
(Mike Weiner)

Detail from promotional poster for ABC's new comedies in the fall 1996 season, including Greg's *Common Law*. *(Wayne Jones)*

Dave Attell and Greg in New York City, May 2009.
(Michelle Paul)

[Below] Mike DeStefano and Greg, June 2009.
(Michelle Paul)

Greg playing guitar, July 2009. *(Michelle Paul)*

Greg checking notes and jokes before his performance at the Bonaroo Music & Arts Festival, Manchester, TN, June 2010. *(Michelle Paul)*

Greg on his Scandinavian tour, 2010.
(Michelle Paul)

[Opposite page top] Greg, David Hasselhoff, and
Jeff Ross at the Comedy Central roast of David
Hasselhoff, 2010. This is the last roast that Greg
performed at before his death. *(Michelle Paul)*

[Opposite page bottom] Greg at a *Last Comic
Standing* taping, 2010. *(Michelle Paul)*

Greg at the Nasty Show of the Montreal
Comedy Festival, July 2010.
(Michelle Paul)

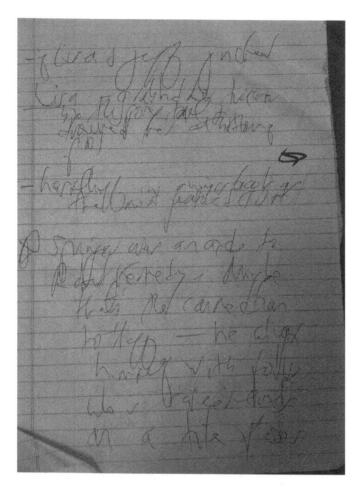

A small sample of Greg's notebooks, including in the one above the infamous joke about Jerry Springer which elicited a shocked groan from some audience members at the roast of David Hasselhoff. *(Michelle Paul)*

Acknowledgments

The authors would like to thank everyone who agreed to be interviewed. There would be no book at all without their openness to talk and their insights into Greg and his work. Thanks to Anthony Gonzalez and Paul Faravhar for their editorial assistance. Special thanks to the UCLA Film & Television Archive (and Manager Mark Quigley) for permission to view the *Common Law* pilot on the archive's VHS copy. We are also very grateful to the people who read early drafts of chapters of the book and offered constructive criticism and feedback: Ashley Balaker, Courtney Balaker, Ted Balaker, Dave Diamond, Pat House, Maureen Jenna, Wayne Johnston, Dave Jones, Ward Jones, Steve Klein, Robert Kurson, Oscar Martens, Beau McFarland, Dennis Regan, Mel Simoneau, and Aaron C. Smith. Thanks to editor Maria Castelli, and to allison calvern for help with proofing. Thank you to Richard McKilligan, Kyle Smith, and Matthew Ritter for their legal insights. And to Angie Sauvé for her work on publicity.

Finally, much appreciation to the backers of this project on Kickstarter. Special recognition goes to: Ashley Balaker, Ted and Courtney Balaker, Joe Bates, Chris Carbone, Miranda Celestre, Scott Damell, Karith Foster, Hilary Fried, Logan Galli, Dan and Gennie Gorback, Barbara Herzinger, Brad

Hutchings, Robert Jadon, Daniel Kantor, Brian Kiley, Jeffrey Leach, Chris Linden, Brett McCabe, Travis McCormack, Bridgette McMahon, Patrick McMullen, Brendon Mulvihill, Luke O'Gara, Linda Patterson, Lou Perez, Robert Prus, Thomas Randall, Teme Ring, Brad Rivers, JR Ryberg, Chad Sabo, Andrew Suydam, Tanya Weiman, and Andrew Wulff. And sincere thanks to: Matt Bedinger, Steven Blackman, Richard Brandes, John Brown, Ronnie Campagnone, Koa Campbell, Carla Hoffman, Maria Castelli, Bill Chivil, Nathan De Leon, Tom Devenport, Dan Dreyer, Aaron Haning, Del Harrison, Scott Holbrook, Jason Johnson, Brian Kaemingk, Cameron Marshall, Matthew MacDougall, Joe McAndrew, Patrick Melton, Matthew Mirapaul, Matt Nevala, Ryan Lee Nevins, Colleen O'Mara, David Owens, Eric Richter, Doug Sidell, Vlad Perelman, Dan Perlman, Jordan Powell, Dave Wellman, and Josh Yates.

Matt: Thanks to Angie, Victor, Greg, Ted, and Courtney Balaker as well as Teri, Lee, and Chelsea Starkweather. None of this would have happened without you. And, of course, my lovely Ashley, you're patient and hot and a selfless mommy to Reid and Lincoln, who provide us with more laughter and entertainment than they'll ever imagine. I love you.

Wayne: Thanks to my caring family and to the great friends I am secularly blessed with for demonstrating such interest and support in the writing of this book. You are all much loved and appreciated.

.

Sources

Original Interviews

This book is chiefly based on original interviews that the authors conducted with people who knew Greg professionally or personally. Some of the interviews were carried out by one author, some by another, and a few by both. The interviews were done mostly by telephone, though some were in person or by email, between fall 2014 and fall 2018, of the following people:

Leslie Adler
Estee Adoram
Ted Alexandro
Jessie Baade
Julian Barba
Eddie Brill
J-L Cauvin
Tom Clark
Marc Cook
Elise Czajkowski
Dave Diamond
Nick Di Paolo Jay
Dixit
Mike Donovan
Rick Dorfman
Noam Dworman
Ray Ellin
Greg Fitzsimmons

Dylan Gadino
Jim Gaffigan
Joel Gallen
Melvin George II
MaryAnn Giraldo
Pauline Glaser
Judy Gold
Steve Hofstetter
Conor Hogan
Dom Irrera
Tom Johnson
Jesse Joyce
Myq Kaplan
Robert Kelly
Andy Kindler
Jessica Kirson
Steve Klein
Robert Kurson

Rob LaZebnik
Natasha Leggero Erik
Lievano
Jim Livio
Marc Maron
Jamie Masada Patrick
Melton Lindsay
Merrill
Art Miller Jr.
Jay Mohr
Donna Moore-
sturgill Jim Norton
Matthew Paroly
Michelle Paul

Gene Pompa
Megyn Price
Colin Quinn
Louis Ramey
Eli Sairs
Joe Schrank
Tom Shillue
Steven Siegel
Nick Swardson
Ildiko Tabori
Patti Vasquez
Mike Weiner
Robin Whitaker
(née Lazarus)

Other Sources

Alexandro, Ted. "'Farewell, Maestro,' by Ted Alexandro." *The Comic's Comic*. Oct. 2, 2010. http://thecomicscomic.com/2010/10/02/farewell-maestro-by-ted-alexandro/ (viewed Nov. 18, 2018).

Altman, Michael E. "Greg Giraldo, comedian and former Harvard Law alumnus, dies." *Flyby*. Oct. 2, 2010. http://www.thecrimson.com/flyby/article/2010/10/2/new-giraldo-brunswick-late/ (viewed Jan. 1, 2017).

Appleton, Dina, and Daniel Yankelevits. *Hollywood dealmaking: Negotiating talent agreements for film, TV and new media.* 2nd ed. New York: Allworth Press, 2010.

Attrino, Anthony G. "Drug users who report overdoses would be protected under law proposed in N.J." *NJ.com.* Aug. 27, 2012. http://www.nj.com/middlesex/index.ssf/2012/08 /drug_users_who_report_overdose.html (viewed Jan. 1, 2017).

Baade, Jessie. "Giraldo's tape." *Under this rock.* Sept. 30, 2010. http://jessiebaadeblog.blogspot.ca/2010/09 /giraldos-tape.html (viewed June 25, 2017).

Baade, Jessie. "Greg Giraldo interview 1994." 1994. YouTube video. Posted by Boston Comedy: Funny Grown Here. Oct. 3, 2010. https://www.youtube.com/watch?v=OaDbQdX7M eQ (viewed Jan. 1, 2017).

Bennington, Ron. "Greg Giraldo: A life in comedy." Podcast audio. *Bennington.* Aug. 20, 2017. https://soundcloud.com/theinterrobang/greg-giraldo-a-life-in-comedy (viewed Oct. 7, 2017).

Berg, Aaron (@aaronbergcomedy). Twitter post. "RIP Greg Giraldo. He had stuff that made comics strive to be better." Sept. 29, 2010, 7:03 p.m. https://twitter.com/aaronbergcomedy/status/2592 5384200 (viewed July 30, 2017).

Bianculli, David. "'Common Law' simply unexceptional." *Daily News.* Sept. 27, 1996. http://www.nydailynews.com/archives/entertain

ment/common-law-simply-unexceptional-article-1.747424 (viewed Jan. 1, 2017).

Boss-Bicak, Shira. "25 years of coeducation." *Columbia College Today*. July/Aug. 2009. https://www.college.columbia.edu/cct/archive/jul_aug09/features1 (viewed May 28, 2018).

Bromley, Patrick. "Stand-up comedy in the 1980s." *ThoughtCo*. Mar. 24, 2017. https://www.thoughtco.com/stand-up-comedy-in-the-1980s-801533 (viewed Apr. 4, 2018).

Brooks, Tim, and Earle Marsh. *The complete directory to prime time network and cable TV shows, 1946–present*. 9th ed. New York: Ballantine Books, 2007.

Byrnes, Brian. "Slick Argentinean staple looks to make trip to U.S." *Hollywood Reporter*. June 23, 2008. http://www.hollywoodreporter.com/news/slick-argentinean-staple-looks-make-114349 (viewed Jan. 1, 2017).

CK, Louis (@louisck). Twitter post. "Greg giraldo was a good guy. The kind of [guy] you're always glad to see. Also a funny comic and person. He died today. Goodbye friend." Sept. 29, 2010, 3:12 p.m. https://web.archive.org/web/20101008032421/https://twitter.com/louisck/status/25921739061 (viewed Oct. 13, 2018).

Collins, Elvis (@elviscollins). Twitter post. "Greg Giraldo was the only one from Last Comic 7 who came out and talked to us on line without a camera following him. A class act. #fb." Sept. 29, 2010, 6:58 p.m.

https://twitter.com/elviscollins/status/2592505742
0 (viewed July 30, 2017).

Columbia University School of Dental and Oral
Surgery. [*Yearbook*]. 1992.
https://archive.org/details/columbiauniv1992colu
(viewed Jan. 1, 2018).

"Comedian Greg Giraldo brings his rising star to
New Jersey and dies." *Morbid New Jersey*. Nov. 16,
2011.
http://morbidnewjersey.com/2011/11/16/greg-
giraldo-dead-of-overdose-in-new-brunswick/
(viewed Jan. 1, 2017).

Czajkowski, Elise. "'It was a fighter's comedy show':
The oral history of 'Tough Crowd with Colin
Quinn.'" *Splitsider*. Sept. 9, 2013.
http://splitsider.com/2013/09/the-oral-history-of-
tough-crowd-with-colin-quinn/ (viewed Jan. 1,
2017).

DiGiacomo, Frank. "Jack Carter smothers brothers
at rip-roaring friars roast." *Observer*. Oct. 13, 2003.
http://observer.com/2003/10/jack-carter-
smothers-brothers-at-riproaring-friars-roast/
(viewed Jan. 1, 2017).

Dixit, Jay. "Greg Giraldo on failure." *Psychology
Today*. May 13, 2009.
https://www.psychologytoday.com/blog
/brainstorm/200905/greg-giraldo-failure (viewed
Jan. 13, 2019).

Dixit, Jay. "Take my life, please." *New York Times*.
Oct. 31, 2004.

https://www.nytimes.com/2004/10/31/nyregion/thecity/take-my-life-please.html (viewed Jan. 13, 2019).

Downs, Gordon. "Interview with comedian Greg Giraldo." *SanDiego.com*. Dec. 1, 2010. http://www.sandiego.com/articles/2010–12–01/interview-comedian-greg-giraldo (viewed Jan. 1, 2017).

Fitzsimmons, Greg (@GregFitzShow). Twitter post. "RIP GREG GIRALDO. ONE OF THE TRULY GREAT COMICS AND GREAT FRIENDS." Sept. 29, 2010, 6:40 p.m. https://twitter.com/GregFitzShow/status/25923715332 (viewed July 30, 2017).

The Fix. "About Us." *The Fix*. https://www.thefix.com/content/about-us (viewed Jan. 1, 2017).

Fretts, Bruce. "Meet the comic who gave Ray Romano a run for his money." *Entertainment Weekly*. Sept. 12, 2003. http://www.ew.com/article/2003/09/12/meet-comic-who-gave-ray-romano-run-his-money (viewed Jan. 1, 2017).

Gacser, Ava. "Greg Giraldo: A (not so) funny thing happened on the way to the comedy club." *Ava Gacser's Blog*. Sept. 26, 2010. https://avagacser.wordpress.com/2010/09/26/greg-giraldo-a-not-so-funny-thing-happened-on-the-way-to-the-comedy-club/ (viewed Jan. 1, 2017).

Gadino, Dylan P. "Comedian friends joke about Greg Giraldo's death at roast." *Laughspin.com.* Nov. 3, 2010. http://www.laughspin.com/comedian-friends-joke-about-greg-giraldos-death-at-roast/ (viewed July 1, 2018).

Gadino, Dylan. "Greg Giraldo: Comedy game plan in effect." *Punchline Magazine.* Dec. 7, 2009. http://punchlinemagazine.tumblr.com/post/27323 6342/greg-giraldo-comedy-game-plan-in-effect (viewed May 21, 2016, but no longer accessible; now accessible at https://archive.li/nxeOn, viewed July 31, 2018).

Gadino, Dylan P. "Greg Giraldo: The never before seen 35-minute video interview [Mar. 24, 2010]." *Laughspin.* Oct. 1, 2010. http://www.laughspin.com/greg-giraldo-the-never-before-seen-35-minute-video-interview/ (viewed Jan. 9, 2017).

Garvey, Marianne. "Jon Stewart, Sarah Silverman, Chris Rock and famous friends send off Greg Giraldo." *E! News.* Oct. 5, 2010. https://www.eonline.com/news/204061/jon-stewart-sarah-silverman-chris-rock-and-famous-friends-send-off-greg-giraldo (viewed Dec. 12, 2018).

Geltner, Ted. "Greg Giraldo sounds off on comedy, college." *The Gainesville Sun.* Oct. 7, 2005. https://www.gainesville.com/news/20051007 /greg-giraldo-sounds-off-on-comedy-college (viewed Dec. 12, 2018).

Giraldo, Greg. *Good day to cross a river*. Comedy Central, 2006.

Giraldo, Greg. "Greg Giraldo illegal aliens." Segment from Comedy Central special. YouTube video. Posted by FreeMusic. Feb. 21, 2016. https://www.youtube.com/watch?v=clHwWa6MDxA (viewed Dec. 12, 2018).

Giraldo, Greg (@greggiraldo). Twitter site. https://twitter.com/greggiraldo (viewed Aug. 5, 2017).

Give it up for Greg Giraldo. Executive producer, Joel Gallen. Comedy Central, 2011.

Greathouse, John. "How Bill Gundfest created the Comedy Cellar." YouTube video. Posted by John Greathouse. Oct. 5, 2013. https://www.youtube.com/watch?v=UkH3-v7o4us (viewed Aug. 22, 2018).

"Greg Giraldo 911 call—'He's not breathing.'" TMZ.com. Oct. 11, 2010. http://www.tmz.com/2010/10/11/greg-giraldo-911-tape-call/ (viewed Jan. 6, 2017).

Haber, Matt. "Seeking sobriety in Brooklyn." *New York Times*. Apr. 6, 2011. http://www.nytimes.com/2011/04/07/fashion/07HIPSTERREHAB.html?_r=0 (viewed Jan. 1, 2017).

Hankinson, Andrew. "An upset at the comedians' table." *The New Yorker*. Aug. 28, 2017. https://www.newyorker.com/magazine/2017/08/28/an-upset-at-the-comedians-table (viewed Apr. 21, 2018).

Hogan, Conor. "Almost famous: Comic Greg Giraldo sits on the brink of stardom." *Time Out New York*. No. 480 (Dec. 9–15, 2004).

The Howard Stern Show. SiriusXM Radio. 2004. "Comedian Greg Giraldo on Howard Stern full interview 2015.mp4." YouTube video. Posted by Gwyn Wilhemina. May 31, 2016. https://www.youtube.com/watch?v=PFKoIENAWms_(viewed July 31, 2018).

The Howard Stern Show. SiriusXM Radio. 2006. "Roasting Gary Dell'abate." YouTube video. Posted by RIPGregGiraldo. July 29, 2011. https://www.youtube.com/watch?v=p83b2YYHHS0 (viewed July 31, 2018).

James, Caryn. "Television: They're celebrities, and you're not." *New York Times*. Feb. 8, 2004. https://www.nytimes.com/2004/02/08/arts/television-they-re-celebrities-and-you-re-not.html (viewed Aug. 8, 2014).

Joyce, Jesse. "Jesse Joyce reveals censored Greg Giraldo jokes." YouTube video. Posted by lizzire. July 1, 2011. https://www.youtube.com/watch?v=NmvBkpqxGIs (viewed Aug. 5, 2017).

Joyce, Jesse. "Jesse Joyce @ the Cringe Humor roast of Jim Florentine." YouTube video. Posted by Jesse Joyce. Sept. 29, 2011. https://www.youtube.com/watch?v=2cFnZ8X2NCE (viewed Dec. 12, 2018).

Katsilometes, John. "In retrospect, Gilbert Gottfried's 9/11 joke was maybe 'too soon.'" *Las Vegas Sun*. Feb. 23, 2011. http://lasvegassun.com/blogs/kats-report/2011/feb/23/retrospect-gilbert-gottfrieds-911-joke-was-maybe-t/ (viewed Dec. 24, 2016).

Kurson, Robert. "Who's killing the great lawyers of Harvard?" *Esquire*. Aug. 2000.

Lafayette, Jon. "A showbiz companion." *Television Week*. Vol. 24, issue 4 (Jan. 24, 2005). Business Source Complete (viewed Oct. 8, 2018).

Lampanelli, Lisa (@LisaLampanelli). Twitter post. "There are no words 2 express what a shame it is 2 lose Greg Giraldo. His smart humor was unparalleled & he will be missed for yrs to come." Sept. 29, 2010, 6:59 p.m. https://twitter.com/LisaLampanelli/status/25925106713 (viewed July 30, 2017).

"'Last Comic Standing' judge Greg Giraldo ODs at party." *Fox News*. Sept. 27, 2010. http://www.foxnews.com/entertainment/2010/09/27/comic-standing-judge-greg-giraldo-ods-party.html (viewed Jan. 1, 2017).

The Late Show with David Letterman. CBS. Aired Mar. 4, 2005.

LaZebnik, Rob. Creator. *Common Law*. Warner Bros. Television, 1996.

Lee, Pete (@peteleetweets). Twitter post. "Greg Giraldo bought me groceries once on the road when I was at my poorest. RIP Greg Giraldo.

#greggiraldo." Sept. 29, 2010, 6:27 p.m.
https://twitter.com/peteleetweets/status/25922761
129 (viewed July 30, 2017).

Lipton, Michael A., Tom Gliatto, Greg Cerio, Allison
Lynn, Dan Jewel, Calvin Baker, Pam Lambert, Peter
Carlin, Stephen M. Silverman, Karen S. Schneider,
and John Toolan. "TV's most fascinating people."
People. Sept. 2, 1996.
http://people.com/archive/cover-story-tvs-most-
fascinating-people-vol-46-no-10/ (viewed Jan. 1,
2017).

Lockwood, Alan R. *Barack O'Liberal: The education of
President Obama*. Alan Lockwood Rachlin, 2012.

Mande, Joe. "Taking one for the team: *The marriage
ref* live taping." *Stereogum*. Apr. 13, 2010.
http://www.stereogum.com/1770190/taking-one-
for-the-team-the-marriage-ref-live-taping/vg-
loc/videogum/ (viewed Jan. 1, 2017).

Martin, Denise. "New shot for old 'Crowd.'" *Daily
Variety*. Apr. 25, 2005. Film & Television Literature
Index (viewed Jan. 1, 2017).

McCarthy, Sean L. "Greg Giraldo biographer Matt
Balaker." *Last Things First*. #97 (June 13, 2016).
http://thecomicscomic.com/2016/06/13/episode-
97-greg-giraldo-biographer-matt-balaker/ (viewed
Aug. 5, 2017).

McCarthy, Sean L. "Greg Giraldo's 'Midlife Vices,'
previewed and reviewed." *The Comic's Comic*. Aug.
14, 2009.
http://thecomicscomic.com/2009/08/14/greg-

giraldos-midlife-vices-previewed-and-reviewed/ (viewed Jan. 1, 2017).

McGlynn, Katla, and Jessica Pilot. "An oral history of the Comedy Cellar." *Vanity Fair*. Mar. 14, 2016. http://www.vanityfair.com/hollywood/2016/03 /comedy-cellar-oral-history (viewed Jan. 1, 2017).

Miller, Stuart. "Gotham's first lady of funny." *Variety*. Nov. 9, 2011. http://variety.com/2011/legit/news/gotham-s-first-lady-of-funny-1118045482/ (viewed Jan. 1, 2017).

Milligan, Patrick. "About Cringe Humor." *Cringe Humor*. http://cringehumor.tumblr.com/about (viewed Jan. 1, 2017).

Milligan, Patrick. "The Greg Giraldo Show pilot taping 4/7/05—Sony Studios." *Cringe Humor*. 2005. https://web.archive.org/web/20050417233056/htt p:/www.cringehumor.net/reviews/giraldo_show_ pilot/(viewed July 24, 2016, but no longer accessible; now accessible at http://archive.is/Vk4II (viewed July 31, 2018).

Milligan, Patrick. "Thank you for the support!" *Cringe Humor*. Oct. 2, 2014. http://cringehumor.tumblr.com/post/99018924427 /thank-you-for-the-support (viewed Jan. 1, 2017).

Morril, Sam (@sammorril). Twitter post. "RIP Greg Giraldo. Not fair to lose such a brave, brilliant and inspiring comedian. http://yfrog.com/5u8g9j." Sept. 29, 2010, 6:37 p.m.

https://twitter.com/sammorril/status/2592353451 9 (viewed July 30, 2017).

New York State Office of Alcoholism and Substance Abuse Services. "Thousands rally in New York City to support those in recovery." *readMedia*. Sept. 22, 2010.
http://readme.readmedia.com/Thousands-Rally-in-New-York-City-to-Support-Those-in-Recovery/1729231 (viewed Jan. 1, 2017).

Norton, Jim (@JimNorton). Twitter post. "Greg Giraldo passed away today. This is the last photo of us together, taken June 28 at Noam's wedding. RIP buddy. http://yfrog.com/497tqrj." Sept. 29, 2010, 4:58 p.m.
https://twitter.com/JimNorton/status/2591665947 5 (viewed July 30, 2017).

O'Connor, Anahad. "Greg Giraldo, insult-humor comic, dies at 44." *New York Times*. Sept. 30, 2010.
http://www.nytimes.com/2010/09/30/arts /30giraldo.html (viewed Jan. 1, 2017).

O'Connor, John J. "A sitcom, upscale and Latin." *New York Times*. Sept. 28, 1996.
http://www.nytimes.com/1996/09/28/arts/a-sitcom-upscale-and-latin.html (viewed Jan. 1, 2017).

OKCable. Television commercial. 2005. "Greg Giraldo & high speed internet (1.800.OKcable)." YouTube video. Posted by 77surfone. Apr. 13, 2013.
https://www.youtube.com/watch?v=IKcHCfEWI1 8 (viewed Jan. 1, 2017).

Opie and Anthony. XM Radio. May [6?], 2009. YouTube video. Posted by Jay832009. Feb. 6, 2011. https://www.youtube.com/watch?v=3gg6hl71vbA (viewed Dec. 26, 2016).

P., Ken. "An interview with Greg Giraldo." *IGN.* June 30, 2004. http://ca.ign.com/articles/2004/06/30/an-interview-with-greg-giraldo (viewed Oct. 28, 2018).

Passoja, Erik (@ErikPassoja). Twitter post. "RIP Greg Giraldo . . . you were an inspiration to all us up-and-coming comics back in the '90's. Wherever you are now, keep 'em laughing. . . ." Sept. 29, 2010, 7:31 p.m. https://twitter.com/ErikPassoja/status/259275931 13. (viewed July 30, 2017).

Politically Incorrect. ABC. Aired Sept. 17, 2001.

Porter, Jane. "Can this man successfully treat opioid addiction with marijuana?" *The Guardian.* Mar. 9, 2017. https://www.theguardian.com/science/2017/mar/09/opioid-addiction-marijuana-treatment-joe-schrank-high-sobriety (viewed June 18, 2017).

Riden, Chad (@ChadRiden). Twitter post. "RIP Greg Giraldo. Thanks for laughing at my stupid jokes & for telling me not to kill myself. You made my LCS audition actually fun." Sept. 29, 2010, 7:41 p.m. https://twitter.com/ChadRiden/status/2592829799 0 (viewed July 30, 2017).

"The Roast of Patrice O'Neal—Full." YouTube video. Posted by comacow02. Aug. 23, 2016.

https://www.youtube.com/watch?v=O3jdBSNQrq
I (viewed Dec. 12, 2018).

Sakulku, Jaruwan, and James Alexander. "The impostor phenomenon." *International Journal of Behavioral Science*. Vol. 6, no. 1 (2011). https://www.sciencetheearth.com/uploads/2/4/6/5/24658156/2011_sakulku_the_impostor_phenomenon.pdf (viewed Sept. 9, 2018).

Schrank, Joe. "Greg Giraldo's last laugh." *The Fix*. Sept. 29, 2011. https://www.thefix.com/content/greg-giraldo-one-year9193?page=all (viewed Jan. 1, 2017).

Serota, Maggie. "Greg Giraldo." *A.V. Club*. Sept. 17, 2009. http://www.avclub.com/article/greg-giraldo-32904 (viewed Jan. 1, 2017).

Silverman, Sarah (@SarahKSilverman). Twitter post. "RIP Greg Giraldo. Belly-laugh hilarious, prolific, good & kind. A thousand oys can't express." Sept. 29, 2010, 5:31 p.m. https://twitter.com/SarahKSilverman/status/25918878587 (viewed July 30, 2017).

Skadden, Arps, Slate, Meagher & Flom. "Steven Siegel." *News*. Mar. 14, 2013. https://www.skadden.com/news-events/steven-spiegel (viewed Jan. 1, 2017, but no longer accessible).

"Spade fronts Tinseltown send-up." *Broadcasting & Cable*. 135.26 (June 27, 2005). Academic OneFile (viewed Oct. 8, 2018).

Stanhope, Doug. *Before turning the gun on himself.* Roadrunner Records, 2012.

Stanhope, Doug. "Giraldo." *DougStanhope.com.* Oct. 1, 2010.
http://www.dougstanhope.com/journal/2010/10/1/giraldo.html (viewed Jan. 1, 2017).

Tattoo Fixation. A&E Network. May 15, 2006. Segment on Vimeo video.
https://vimeopro.com/idiotbox/idiot-box-productions/video/1576317 (viewed Jan. 5, 2017).

"The 10 best comedy albums of 2009." *Punchline.* Dec. 9, 2009.
http://www.laughspin.com/punchline-magazine-presents-the-10-best-comedy-albums-of-2009/ (viewed June 25, 2017).

"*Tough Crowd with Colin Quinn.*" Wikipedia.
https://en.wikipedia.org/wiki/Tough_Crowd_with_Colin_Quinn (viewed Sept. 16, 2017).

Ward, Kate. "Greg Giraldo: Remembering the great insult comedian." *Entertainment Weekly.* Sept. 30, 2010.
http://www.ew.com/article/2010/09/30/greg-giraldo-death (viewed Jan. 1, 2017).

Weinstein, Steve. "Something uncommon about 'Law.'" *Los Angeles Times.* Oct. 12, 1996.
http://articles.latimes.com/1996–10–12/entertainment/ca-53202_1_common-law (viewed Jan. 1, 2017).

Winfrey, Oprah. "Oprah recruits crackheads for Obama vote!" Segment of interview by ABC News,

Nov. 4, 2008. YouTube video. Posted by vargasmart. Nov. 5, 2008. https://www.youtube.com/watch?v=KPFvhInSw0U (viewed Jan. 1, 2017).

Index

Index

About the Authors

Matt Balaker
is a comic, writer, and former investment fund manager. He lives in Southern California with his two boys and one wife.

Wayne Jones
is a standup comedy fan and academic librarian in Ottawa, Canada. He has written two novels, and a book about personal minimalism called *Less*.